BEGINNING GAMES

Once Upon a Time

Reading Games for Beginning Sounds and First Words

by Marilynn G. Barr

_____
Child's Name

can recognize and
name beginning and
ending sounds.

_____   _____
Date   Teacher

LAB201312
Beginning Games
ONCE UPON A TIME
by Marilynn G. Barr

Published by: Little Acorn Books™
Originally published by: Monday Morning Books, Inc.

Entire contents copyright © 2014 Little Acorn Books™

Little Acorn Books
PO Box 8787
Greensboro, NC 27419-0787

Promoting Early Skills for a Lifetime™

Little Acorn Books™
is an imprint of Little Acorn Associates, Inc.

http://www.littleacornbooks.com

Permission is hereby granted to reproduce student materials in this book for non-commercial individual or classroom use. *School-wide or system-wide use is expressly prohibited.

ISBN 978-1-937257-47-7

Printed in the United States of America

Once Upon a Time

Contents

Introduction 4	There's a Mouse in the House 41
Row, Row, Row Your Boat 5	Game Board 42
Game Board 6	Mouse Game Cards 44
Game Cards 8	Cover 45
Cover 10	Mud Puddle Piglets 46
A Snail's Trail 11	Cover 47
Cover 12	Game Board 48
Game Board 13	Game Cards 50
Game Cards 15	The King's Crowns 52
Once Upon a Time 17	Cover 53
Game Board 18	Game Board 54
Game Cards 20	Jewel Bands and Game Cards 56
Cover 22	Can Stackers 58
Rub-a-Dub-Dub 23	Game Board 59
Game Board 24	Game Cards 61
Tub Patterns and Soap Bar Game Cards 25	
Mittens For Octopus 29	
Game Board 30	
Game Cards 32	
Pin A Tail On A Whale 36	
Game Board and Title 37	
Whale Patterns 38	
Game Cards 40	

Once Upon a Time

Introduction

Introduce early learners to reading with the ready-to-use beginning games featured in *Once Upon a Time*. Children practice recognizing and matching beginning sounds to alphabet pictures as they play trail, match board, clothespin, and stacker games. Every game includes a two-page game board and programmed playing pieces. Game formats also offer fair-play, fine-motor, and memory skills practice.

Children match alphabet pictures to beginning sound letters as they move pawns along Row, Row, Row Your Boat, A Snail's Trail, and Once Upon a Time trail games. Rub-a-Dub-Dub, Mittens For Octopus, and Pin A Tail On A Whale clothespin games offer first word recognition practice as well as fine motor skills development. Children clip tub, mitten, and whale tail clothespin game cards to matching spaces on each clothespin game board. Children place matching letters or words on crowns, cheese wedges, and mud puddles as they play The King's Crowns, There's a Mouse in the House, and Mud Puddle Piglets match board games. Can Stackers offers self-checking multi-dimensional skills practice as children identify and stack matching block game cards.

Once Upon a Time Tic-Tac-Toe For Two Players

Reproduce, color, and cut apart the game board and cards. Each player chooses the cat or dog cards. In turn, each player places a card on one of the spaces. The first player with three cats or dogs in a row, vertically, horizontally, or diagonally, wins.

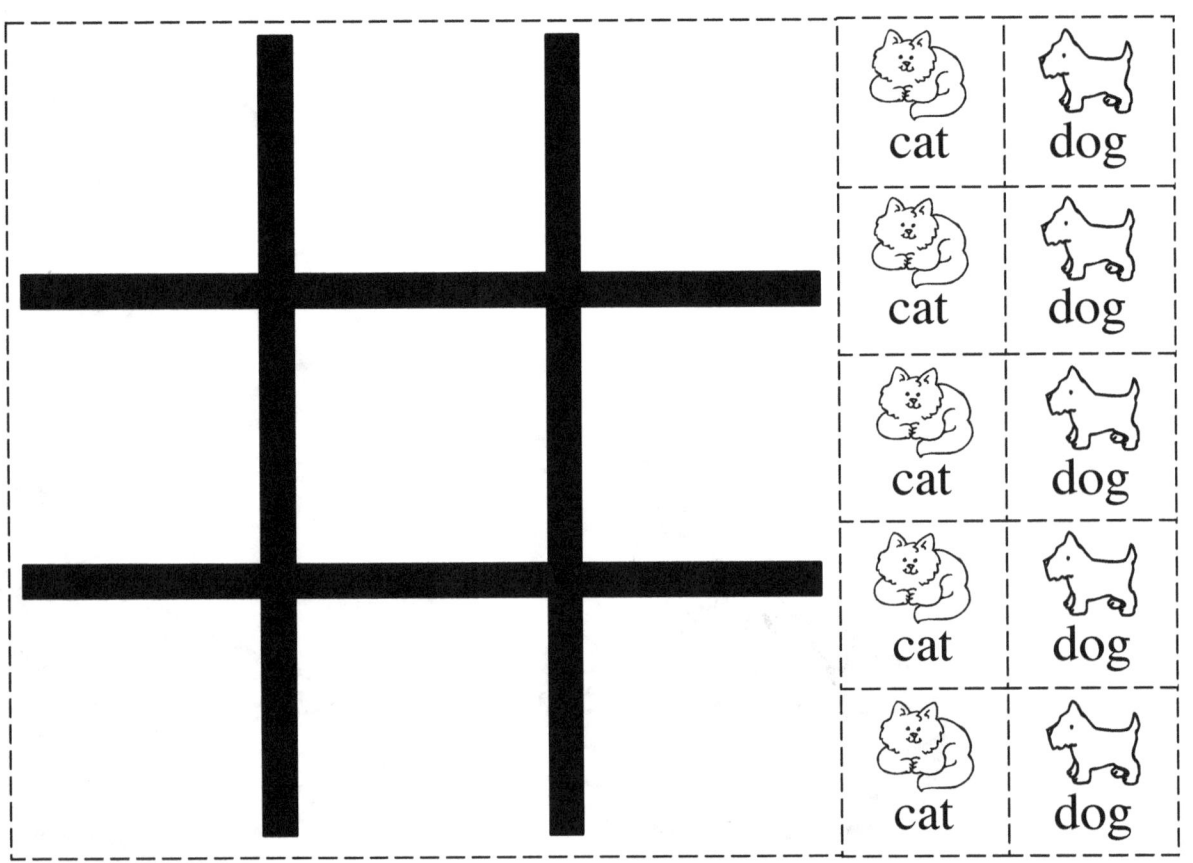

Row, Row, Row Your Boat
A Trail Game
For Two to Four Players

Materials
crayons, markers, scissors, glue, file folder, envelope, tape

Assembly
Game Board: Reproduce, color, and cut out the cover and game board patterns. Matching in the center, glue the game board patterns to the inside of a folder. Glue the cover to the front of the folder, then laminate. Tape an envelope to the back of the game board folder to store pawns and game cards.

Pawns: Reproduce, color, laminate, and cut out a set of pawns. Store the pawns in the envelope on the back of the folder.

Game Cards: Reproduce, color, laminate, then cut out one set of the beginning sound oar or ending sound life preserver game cards. Option: Reproduce, color, and glue each page of cards to the back of a sheet of gift wrap, then laminate, and cut apart the cards. Store the game cards in the envelope on the back of the game board folder.

How to Play
Set up the game board and a matching set of beginning sound oars or ending sound life preservers on a table. Tell children if the game is a beginning or ending sound activity. Each player chooses a pawn. Then one player shuffles and places the deck of shape cards, face down, on the table. Each player, in turn, draws a card, identifies the beginning or ending sound, and moves his or her pawn to the next matching space on the game board. Drawn cards are placed, face down, in a discard pile. Play continues until each player reaches land. When all the cards have been drawn, reshuffle the discard pile and continue playing.

Row, Row, Row Your Boat Game Board

Row, Row, Row Your Boat

Help the animals row, row, row their boats to land.

Start

Row, Row, Row Your Boat Game Board

C T D G H B L

The End

Oar Game Cards
Beginning Sounds

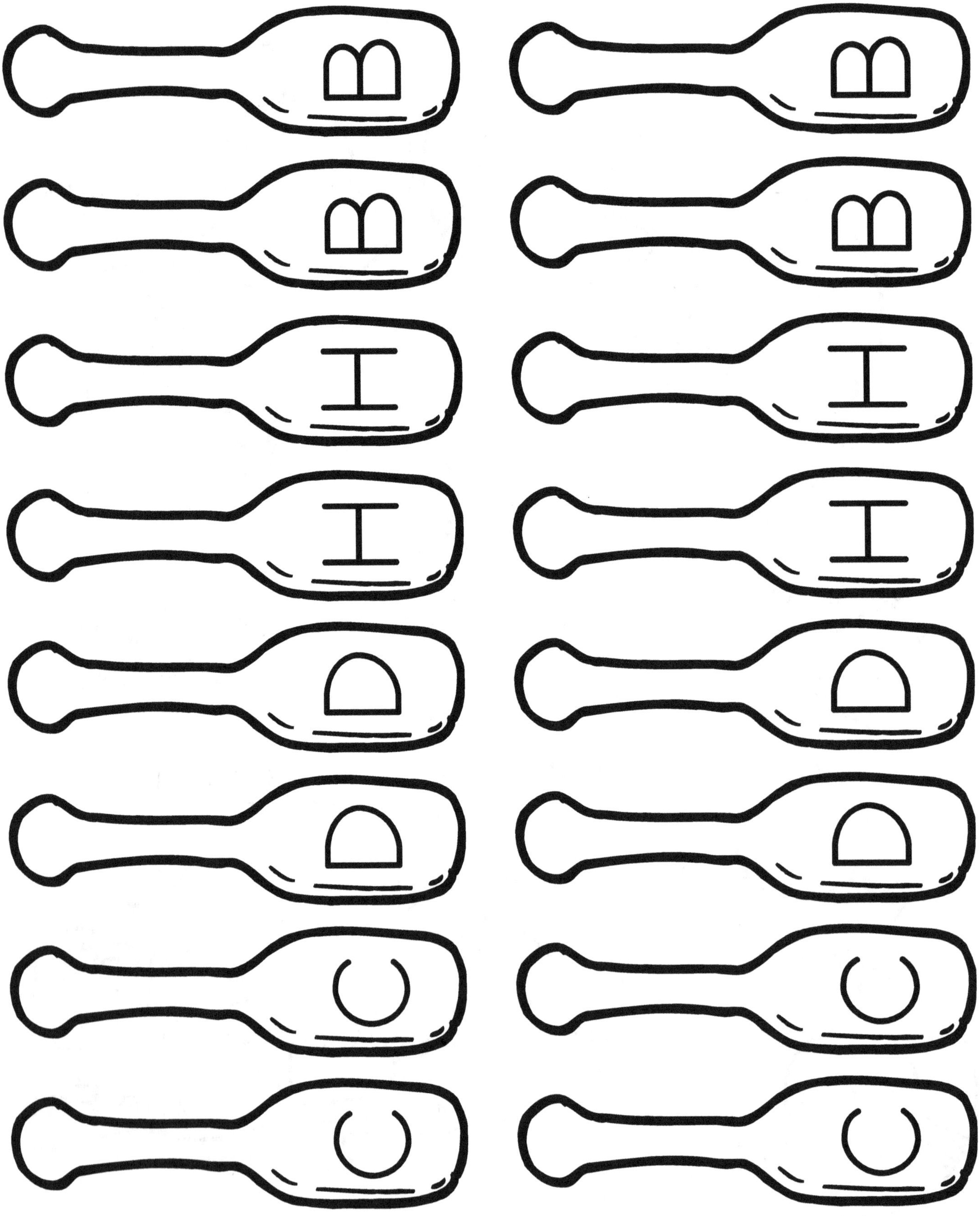

Reproduce, color, laminate, then cut out one set of game cards.

Life Preserver Game Cards
Ending Sounds

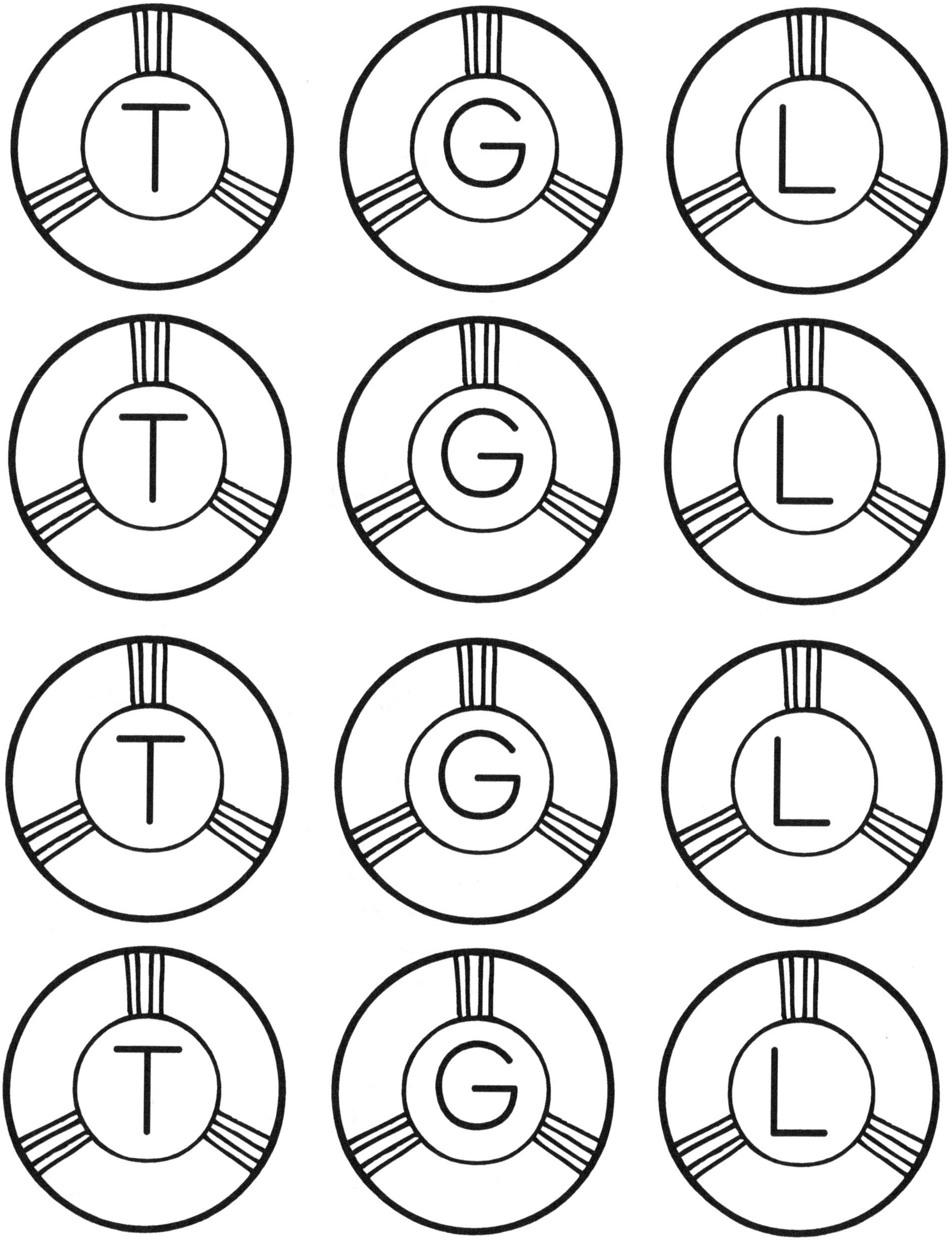

Reproduce, color, laminate, then cut out one set of game cards.

Row, Row, Row Your Boat Cover

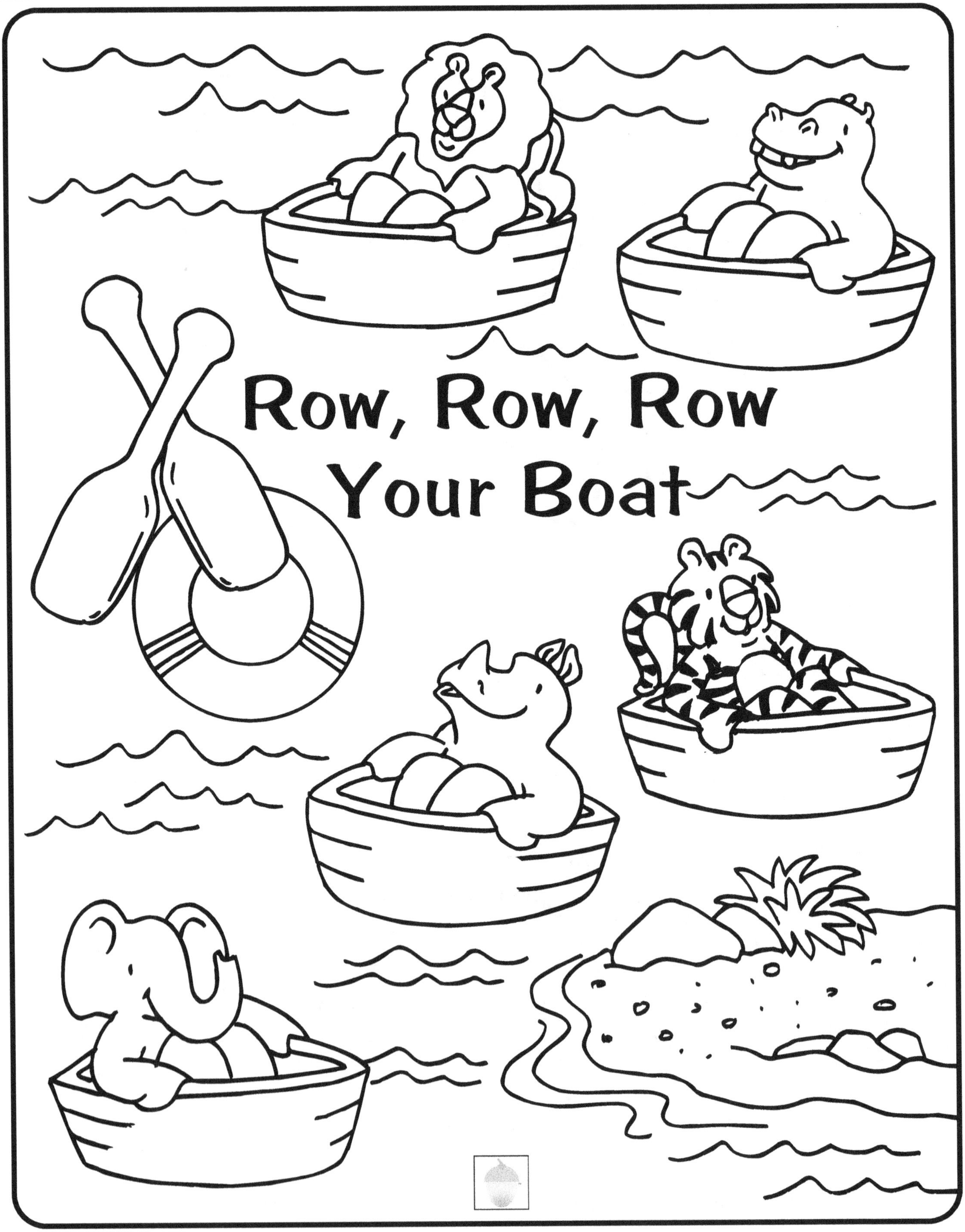

A Snail's Trail
A Trail Game
For Two to Four Players

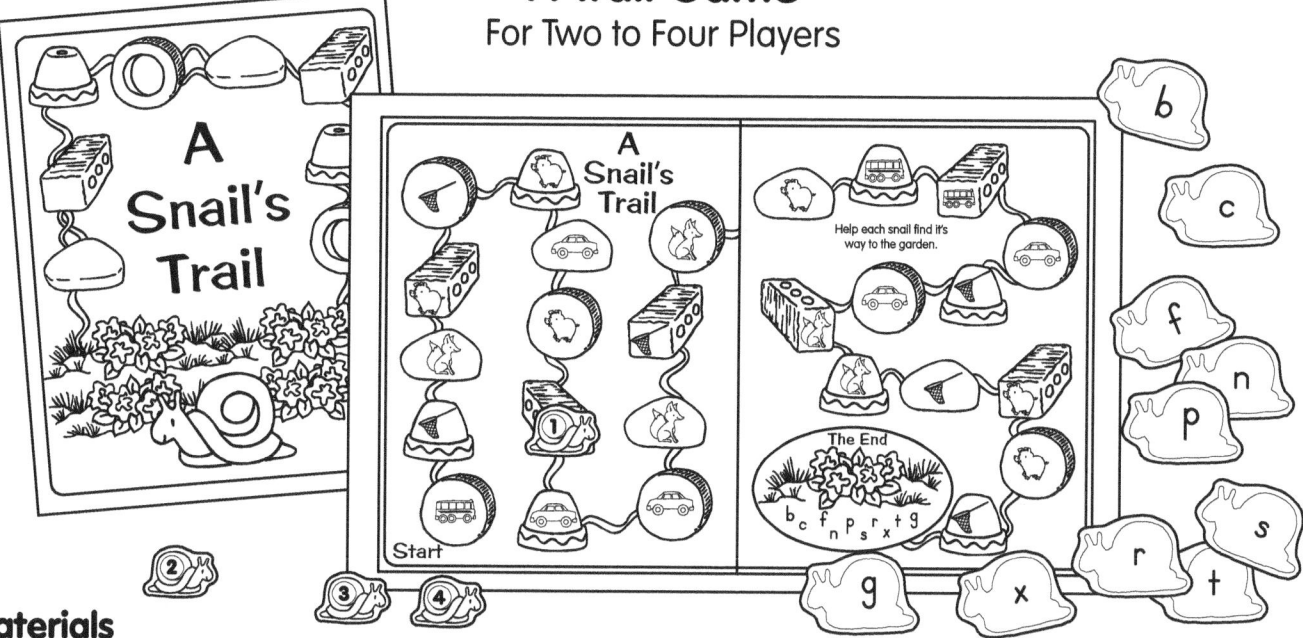

Materials
crayons, markers, scissors, glue, file folder, envelope, tape

Assembly
Game Board: Reproduce, color, and cut out the cover and game board patterns. Matching in the center, glue the game board patterns to the inside of a folder. Glue the cover to the front of the folder, then laminate. Tape an envelope to the back of the game board folder to store pawns and game cards. Note: Make two game boards, one for beginning and one for ending sounds practice.

Pawns: Reproduce, color, laminate, and cut out a set of pawns. Store the pawns in the envelope on the back of the folder.

Game Cards: Reproduce, color, laminate, then cut out a set of beginning sound or ending sound game cards. Option: Reproduce, color, and glue each page of cards to the back of a sheet of gift wrap, then laminate and cut out the cards. Store the game cards in the envelope on the back of the game board folder. (Include a mix of beginning and ending sound snail cards for advanced players.)

How to Play
Set up the game board and cards on a table. Each player chooses a pawn. Then one player shuffles and places the snail cards, face down, on the table. Each player, in turn, draws a card and moves his or her pawn to the next matching space on the game board. Drawn cards are placed, face down, in a discard pile. Play continues until each player reaches the garden at The End. When all the cards have been drawn, reshuffle the discard pile and continue playing.

Pawns

A Snail's Trail Cover

A Snail's Trail Game Board

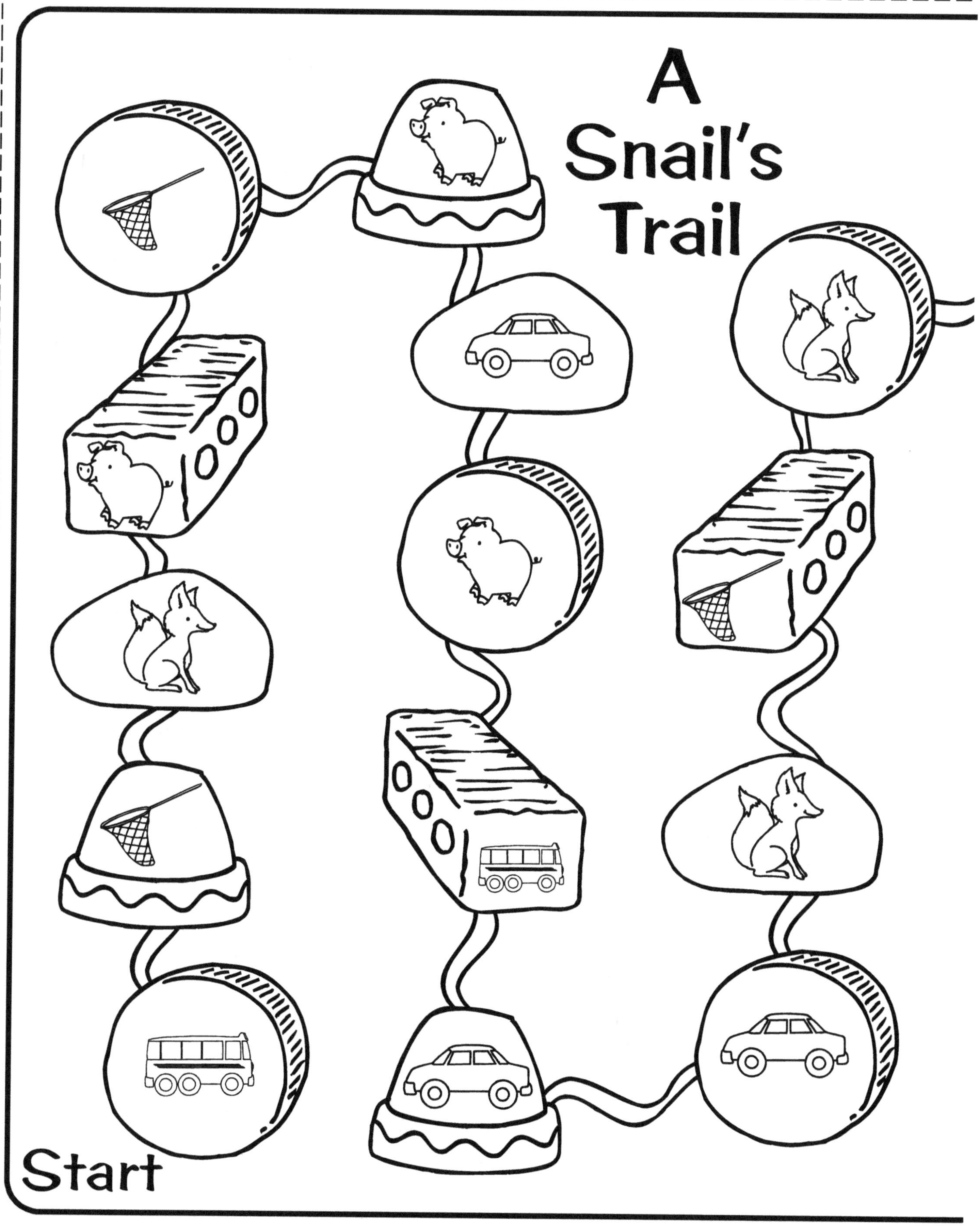

A Snail's Trail

Start

A Snail's Trail Game Board

Snail Game Cards
Beginning Sounds

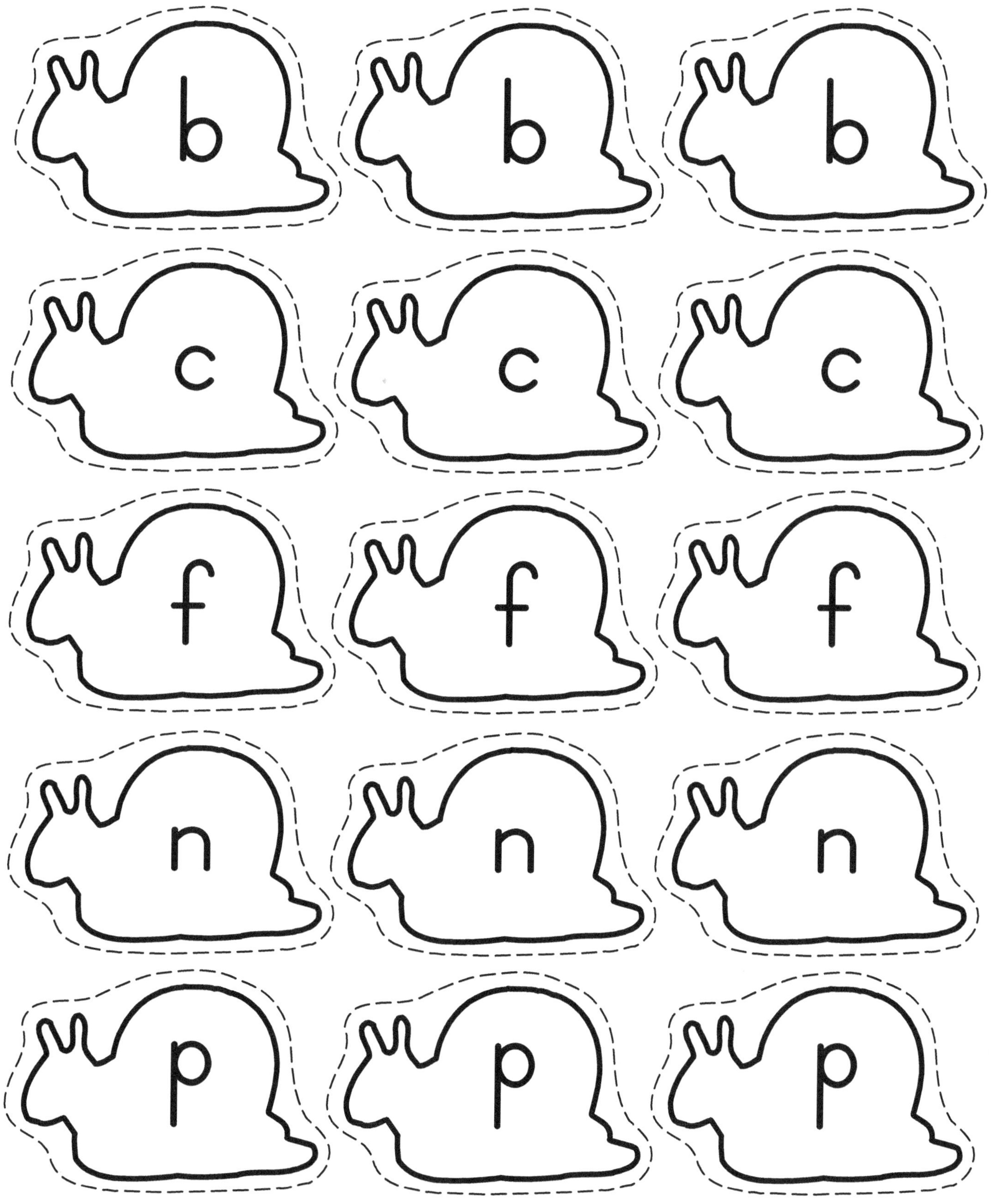

Reproduce, color, and cut out one set of game cards.

Snail Game Cards
Ending Sounds

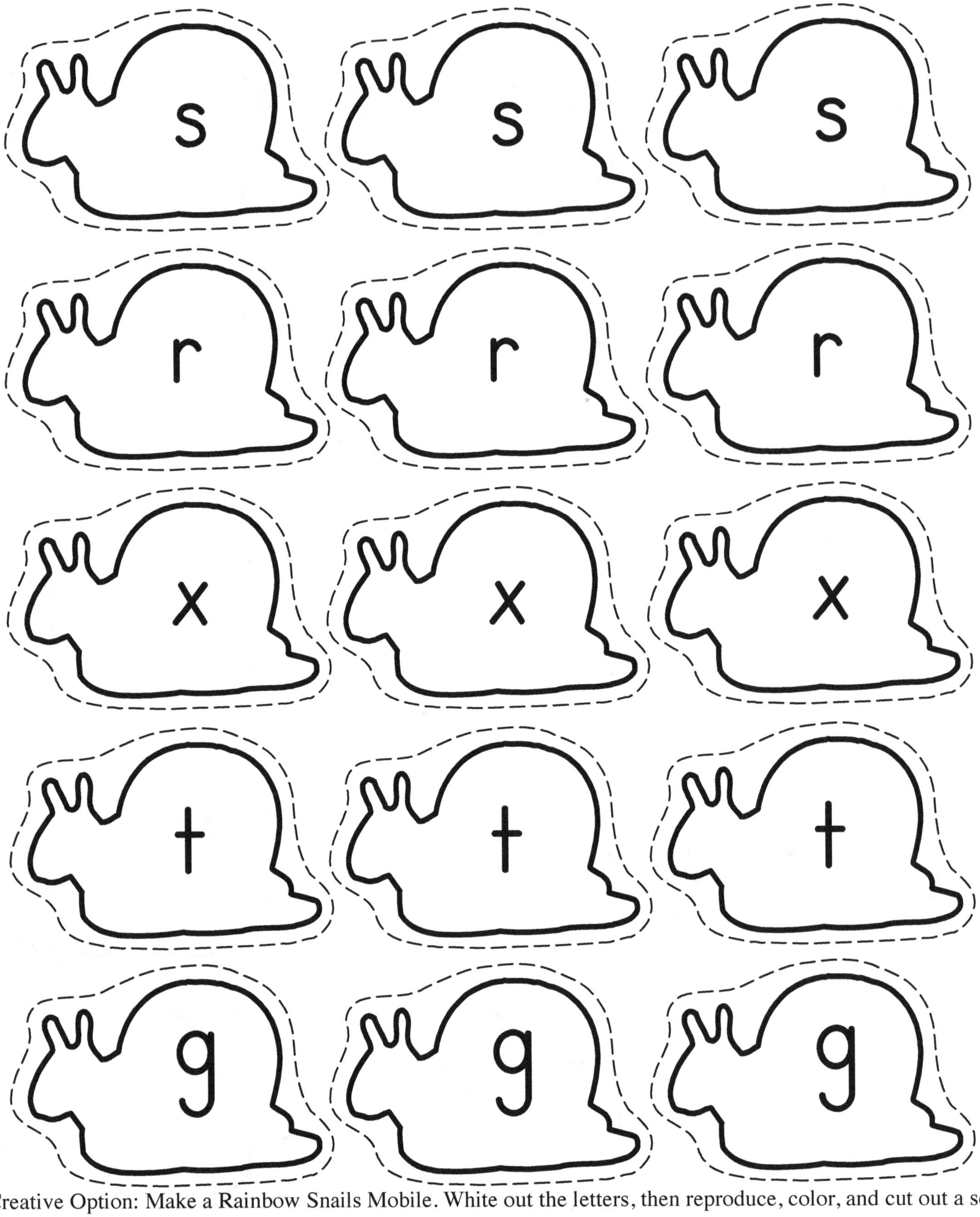

s	s	s
r	r	r
x	x	x
t	t	t
g	g	g

Creative Option: Make a Rainbow Snails Mobile. White out the letters, then reproduce, color, and cut out a set of game cards. Add features to each snail. Punch a hole, then tie a length of yarn at the top of each snail. Tie the loose ends of yarn to a hanger to form a mobile.

Once Upon a Time
A Trail Game
For Two to Four Players

Pawns

Materials
crayons, markers, scissors, glue, file folder, envelope, tape

Assembly
Game Board: Reproduce, color, and cut out the cover and game board patterns. Matching in the center, glue the game board patterns to the inside of a folder. Glue the cover to the front of the folder, then laminate. Tape an envelope to the back of the game board folder to store pawns and game cards. Note: Make two game boards, one for beginning and one for ending sounds practice.

Pawns: Reproduce, color, laminate, and cut out a set of pawns. Store the pawns in the envelope on the back of the folder.

Game Cards: Reproduce, color, laminate, then cut out two sets of game cards. Option: Reproduce, color, and glue each page of cards to the back of a sheet of gift wrap, then laminate and cut out the cards. Store the game cards in the envelope on the back of the game board folder. (Include a mix of beginning and ending sound crown cards for advanced players.)

How to Play
Set up the game board and beginning or ending sound crown cards on a table. Each player chooses a pawn. Then one player shuffles and places the crown cards, face down, on the table. Each player, in turn, draws a card and moves his or her pawn to the next matching space on the game board. Drawn cards are placed, face down, in a discard pile. Play continues until each player reaches the castle keep at The End. When all the cards have been drawn, reshuffle the discard pile and continue playing.

Once Upon a Time Game Board

Once Upon a Time Game Board

Follow the stone path to the castle keep.

The End

o j w
b j s
t l x
r x g

Crown Game Cards
Beginning Sounds

Reproduce, color, and cut out two sets of game cards.

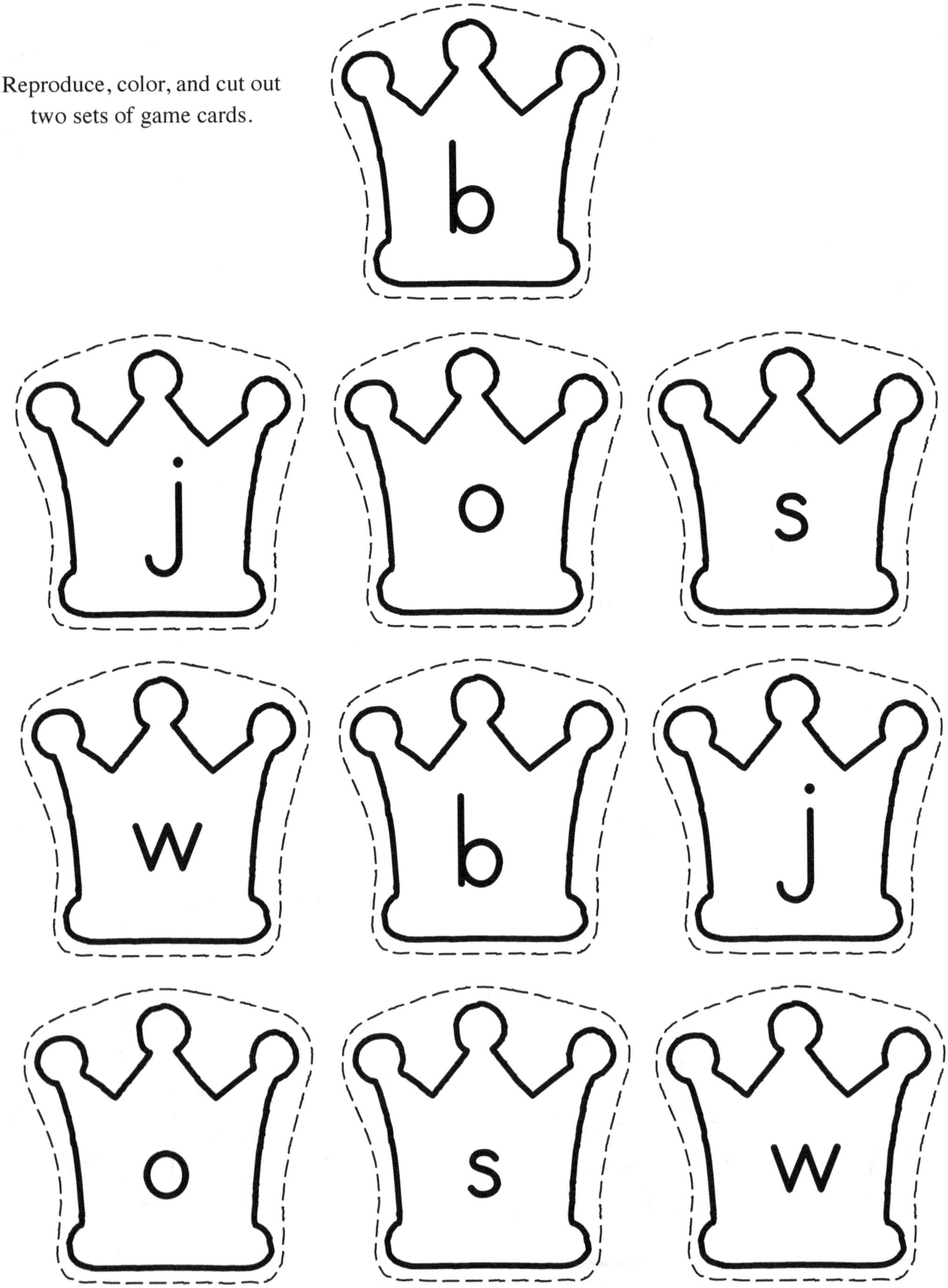

b

j   o   s

w   b   j

o   s   w

Crown Game Cards
Ending Sounds

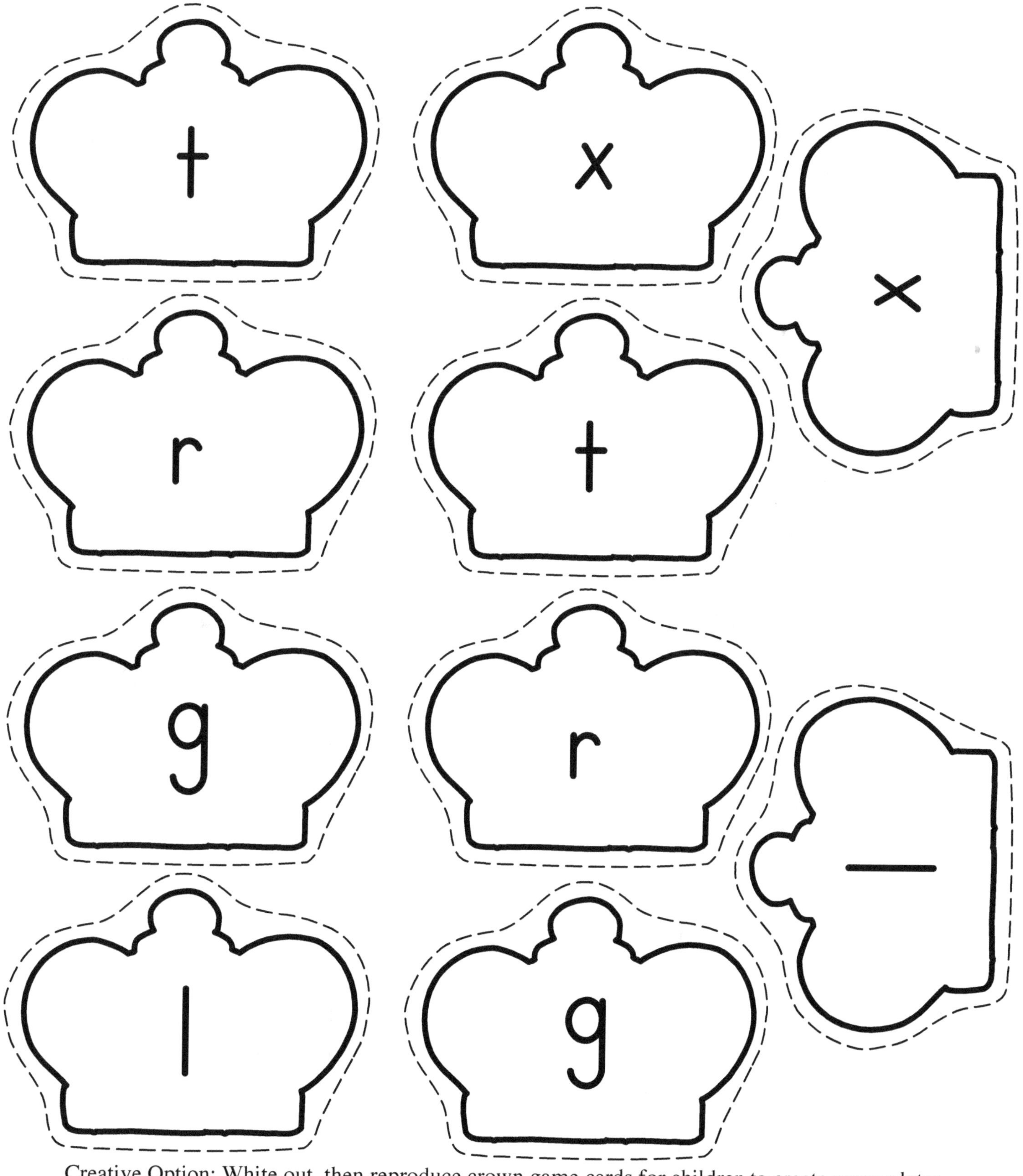

t   x   x

r   t

g   r   —

l   g

Creative Option: White out, then reproduce crown game cards for children to create name plates. Have children color, then cut out the same number of crowns as letters in their individual names. Help each child write a letter on each crown, then assemble the crowns in spelling order on an oak tag sentence strip. Mount the name plates on a display board.

Once Upon a Time Cover

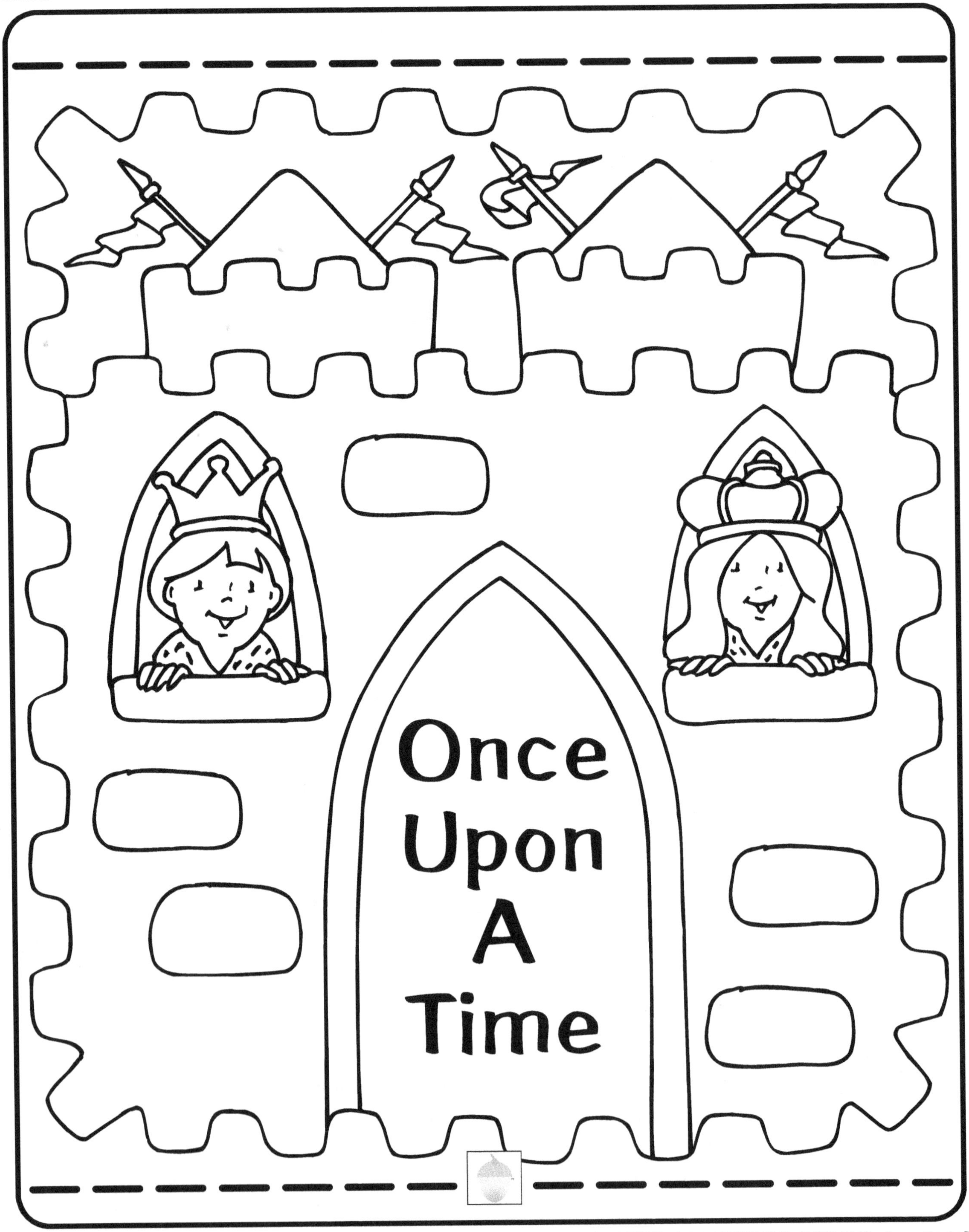

Once
Upon
A
Time

Rub-a-Dub-Dub
A Clothespin Game
For Two Players

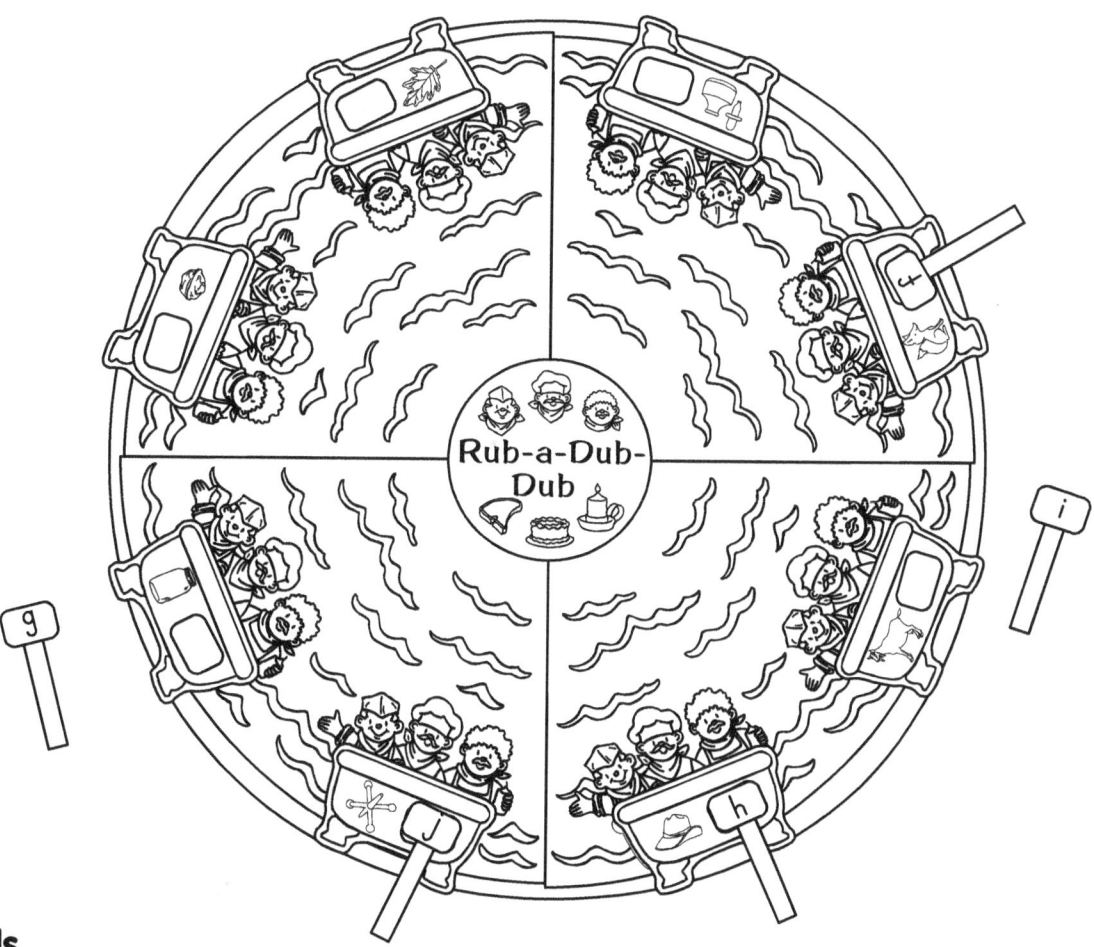

Materials
crayons, markers, scissors, glue, file folders, clothespins, large envelope

Assembly
Game Board: Reproduce, color, and cut out four game board patterns. Matching along the straight edges, glue the game board patterns on a poster board circle to form a round game board. Glue the title in the center of the game board. Then reproduce, color, cut out, and glue eight tub patterns on the assembled game board. Note: Create multiple game boards to focus on different beginning and ending sounds.

Clothespin Game Cards: Reproduce, color, and cut out a set of soap bar game cards. Glue a clothespin to the back of each game card. Decorate a large envelope with soap advertisements and magazine cutouts. Store the clothespin game cards in the envelope.

How to Play
Set up the game board on a table. Place the clothespin game cards, face down, on the table. Each player, in turn, draws a clothespin. If there is a match, the player identifies the match, and clips the clothespin to the correct tub. If there is no match, the player places the clothespin back on the table, face down. Play continues until a soap bar is attached to each matching tub on the game board.

Rub-a-Dub-Dub Game Board and Title

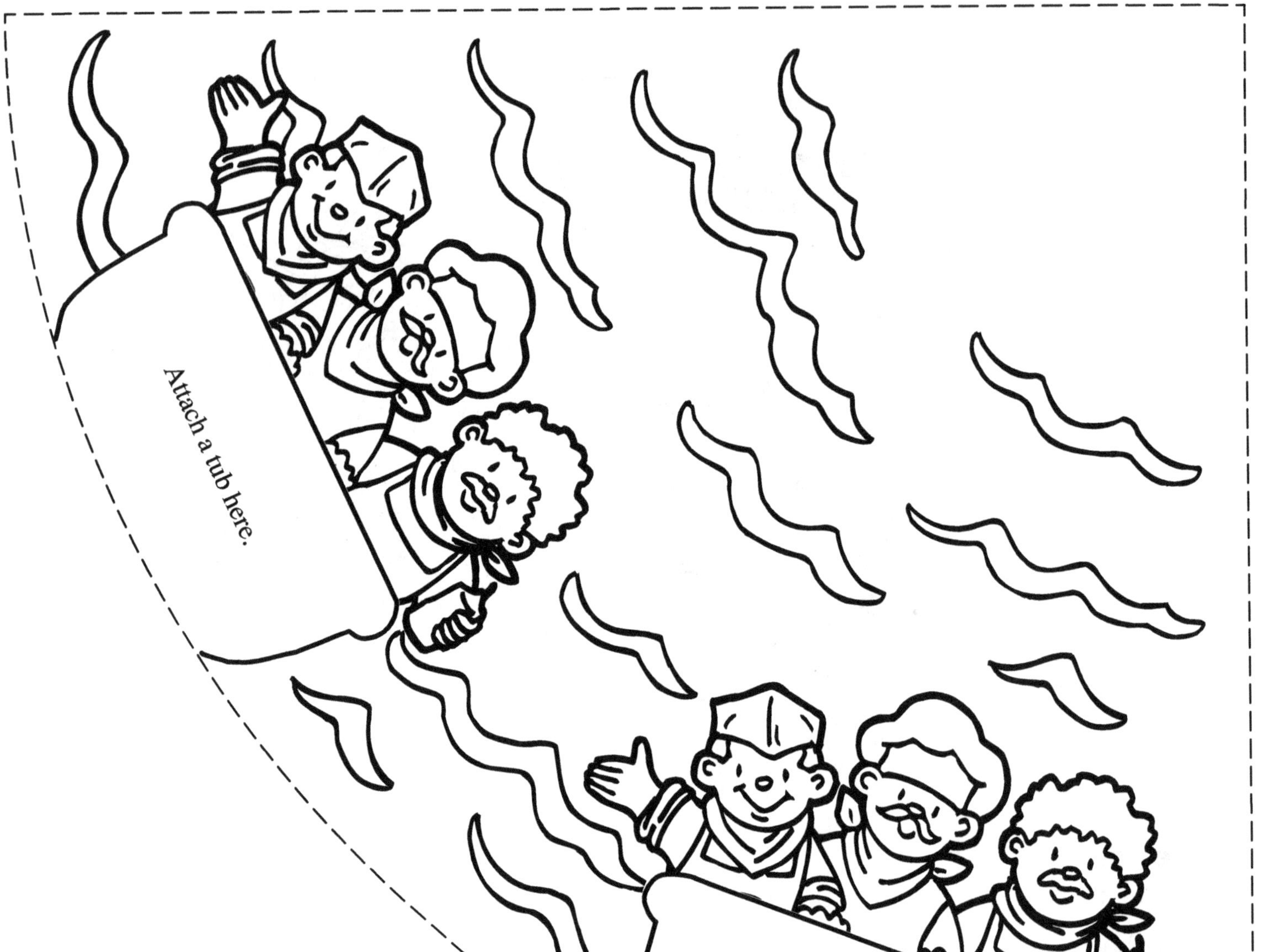

Attach a tub here.

Attach a tub here.

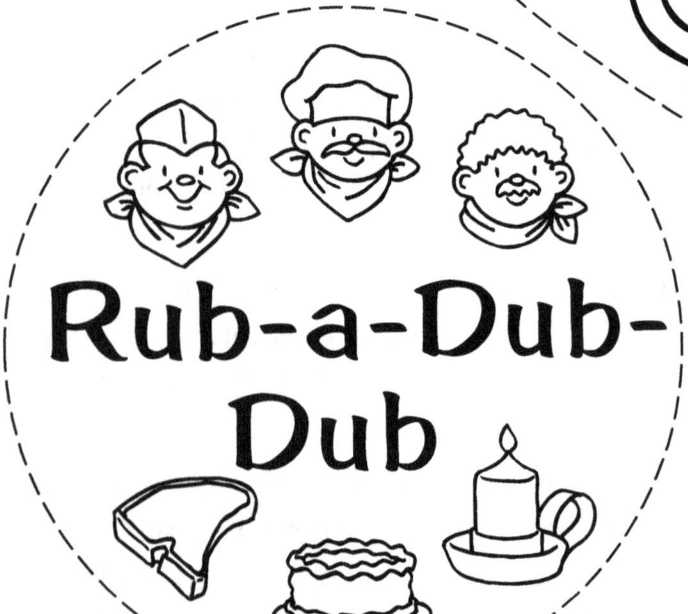

Rub-a-Dub-Dub

Reproduce, color, cut out, and assemble four game board patterns on a poster board circle to form a round game board. Glue the title in the center of the game board.

Tub Patterns and Soap Bar Game Cards

Beginning Sounds

b
b
c
c
d
d
e
e

Reproduce, color, and cut out eight tub patterns. Glue the tub patterns around an assembled Rub-a-Dub-Dub game board.

Ending Sounds

| l | l | t | r |
| l | g | g | r |

LAB201312 • ONCE UPON A TIME • 978-1-937257-47-7 • © 2014 Little Acorn Books™

25

Tub Patterns and Soap Bar Game Cards

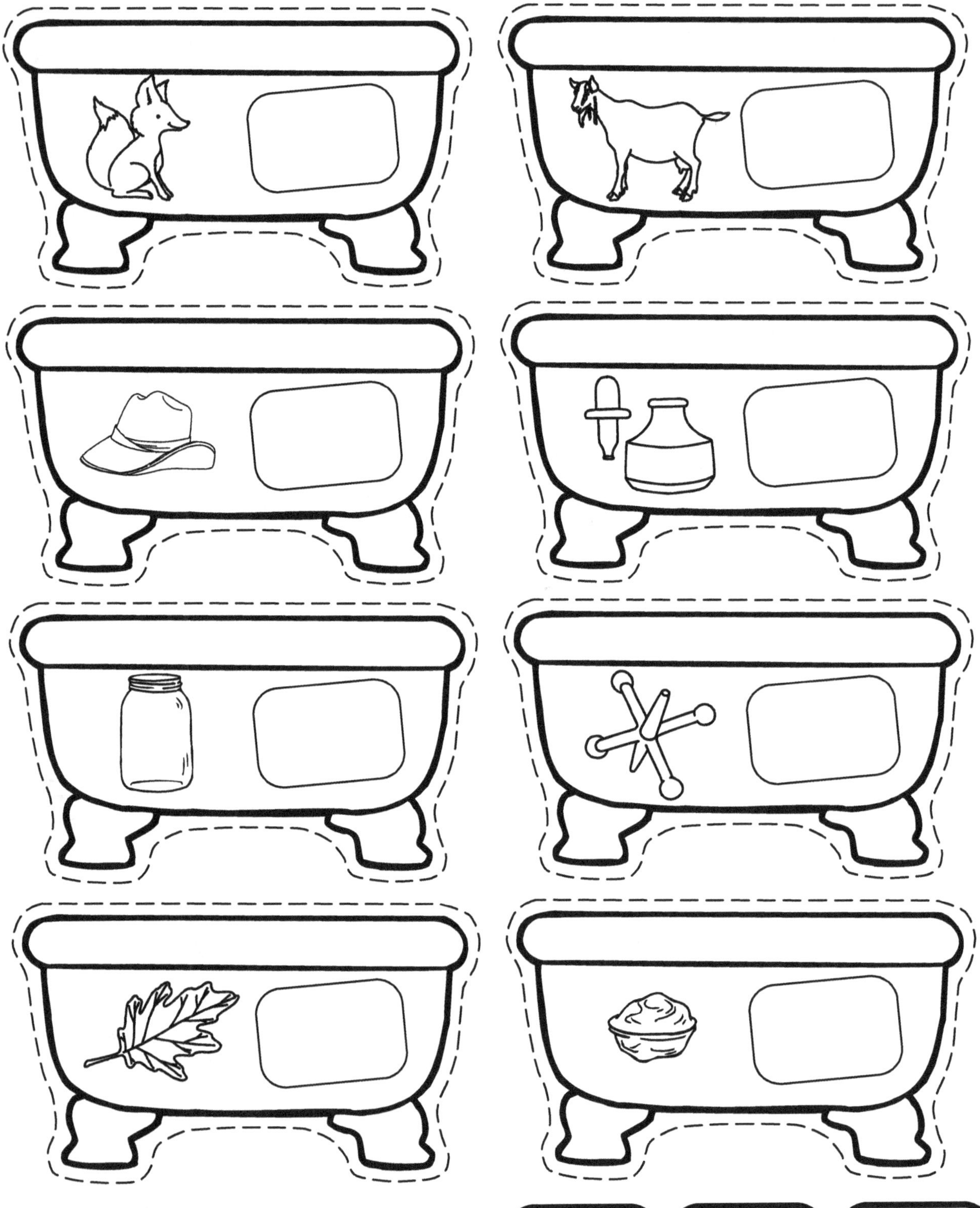

Beginning Sounds

f
g
h
i
j
j
l
n

Reproduce, color, and cut out eight tub patterns. Glue the tub patterns around an assembled Rub-a-Dub-Dub game board.

Ending Sounds

| x | t | t | k |
| r | k | f | t |

Tub Patterns and Soap Bar Game Cards

Beginning Sounds

m
f
s
d
s
b
w
w

Reproduce, color, and cut out eight tub patterns. Glue the tub patterns around an assembled Rub-a-Dub-Dub game board.

Ending Sounds

n g x m
n d b g

Tub Patterns and Soap Bar Game Cards

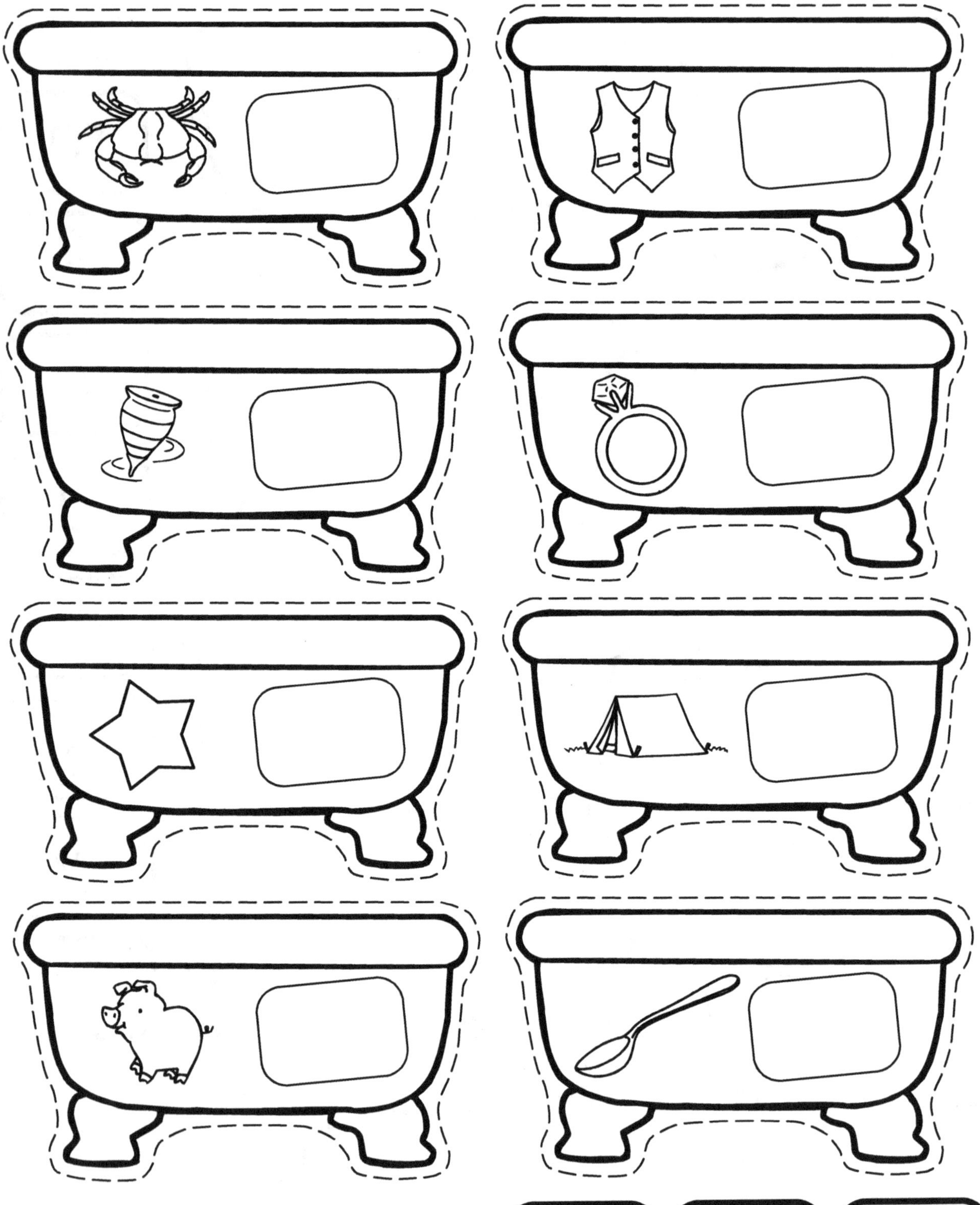

Beginning Sounds

c
v
t
r
s
t
p
s

Reproduce, color, and cut out eight tub patterns. Glue the tub patterns around an assembled Rub-a-Dub-Dub game board.

Ending Sounds

| b | t | p | g |
| r | t | g | n |

Mittens For Octopus
A Clothespin Game
For Two Players

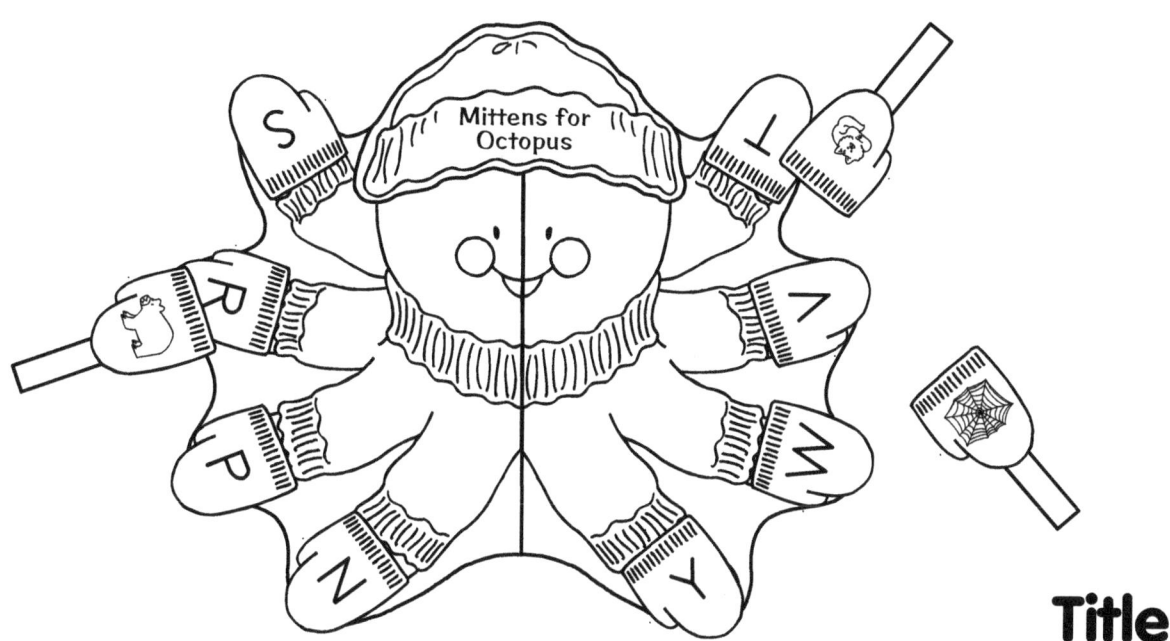

Title

Materials
crayons, markers, scissors, glue, file folders, clothespins, large envelope

Assembly
Game Board: Reproduce, color, and cut out the game board patterns. Matching along the straight edges, glue the game board patterns on a poster board circle to form an octopus. Reproduce, color, cut out, and glue eight beginning or ending sound mittens on the octopus. Note: Make four game boards to use the two sets of beginning and two sets of ending sound mittens.

Clothespin Game Cards: Reproduce, color, and cut out a set of alphabet picture game cards. Glue a clothespin to the back of each game card. Decorate a large envelope with mitten game cards. Store the clothespin game cards in the envelope.

How to Play
Set up the game board on a table. Place the clothespin game cards, face down, on the table. Each player, in turn, draws a clothespin. If there is a match, the player identifies the match, and clips the clothespin to the correct letter mitten. If there is no match, the player places the clothespin back on the table, face down. Play continues until the octopus has a complete set of matching mittens.

Mittens for Octopus Game Board

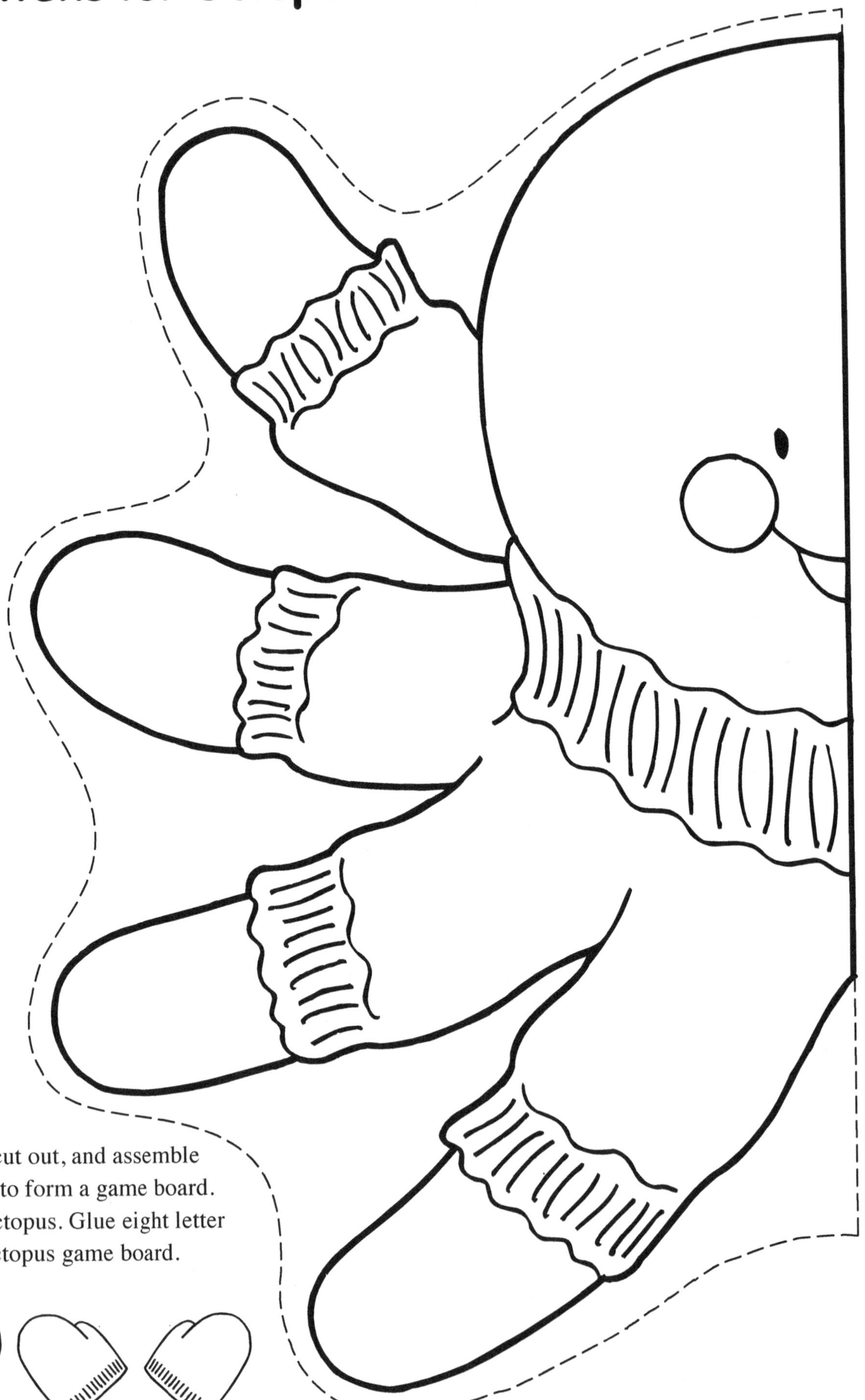

Reproduce, color, cut out, and assemble the octopus patterns to form a game board. Glue the hat on the octopus. Glue eight letter mittens on the octopus game board.

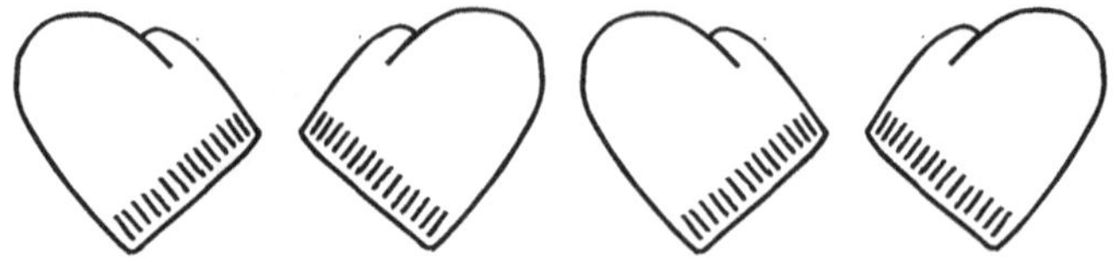

Mittens for Octopus Game Board

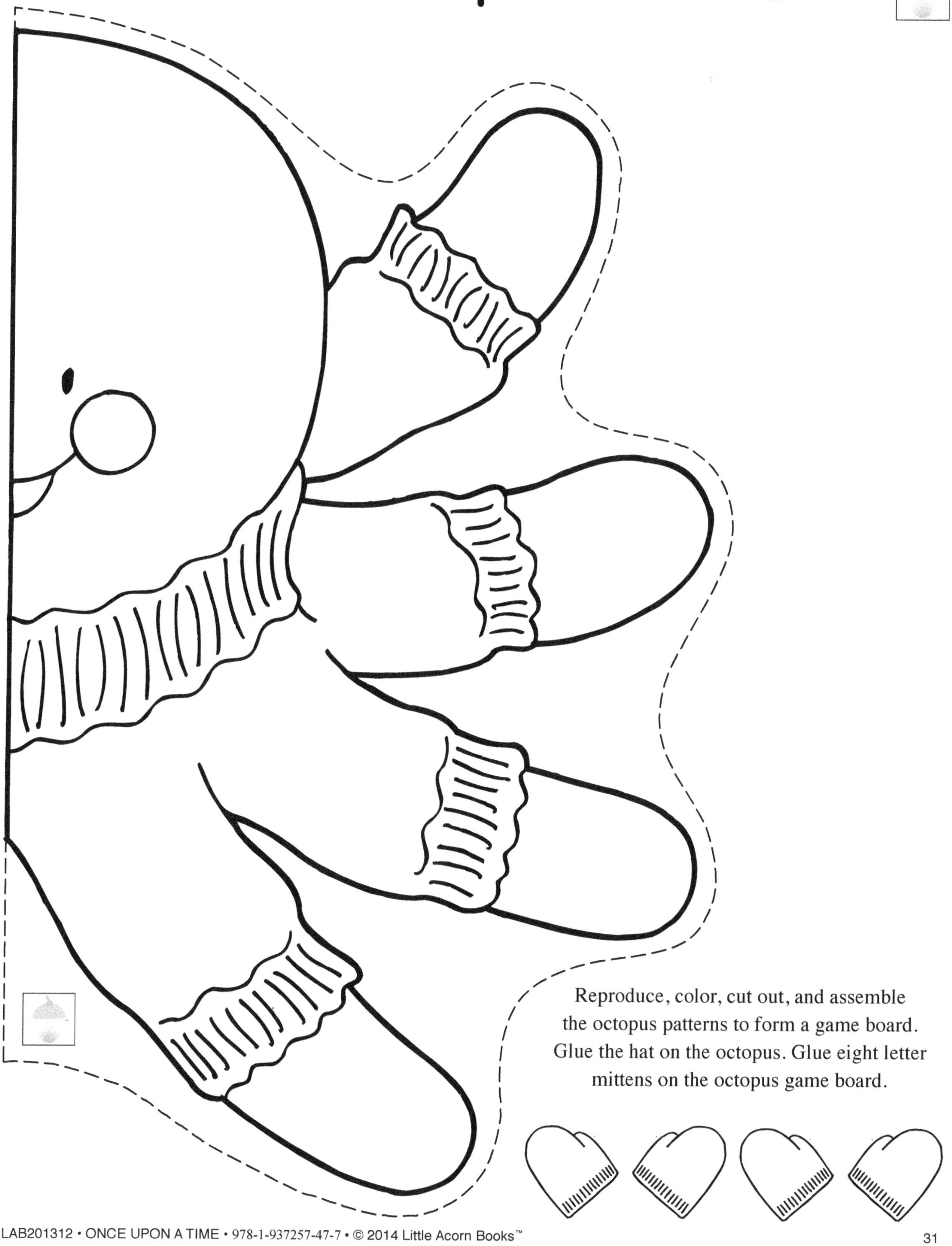

Reproduce, color, cut out, and assemble the octopus patterns to form a game board. Glue the hat on the octopus. Glue eight letter mittens on the octopus game board.

Mitten Game Cards

Beginning Sounds

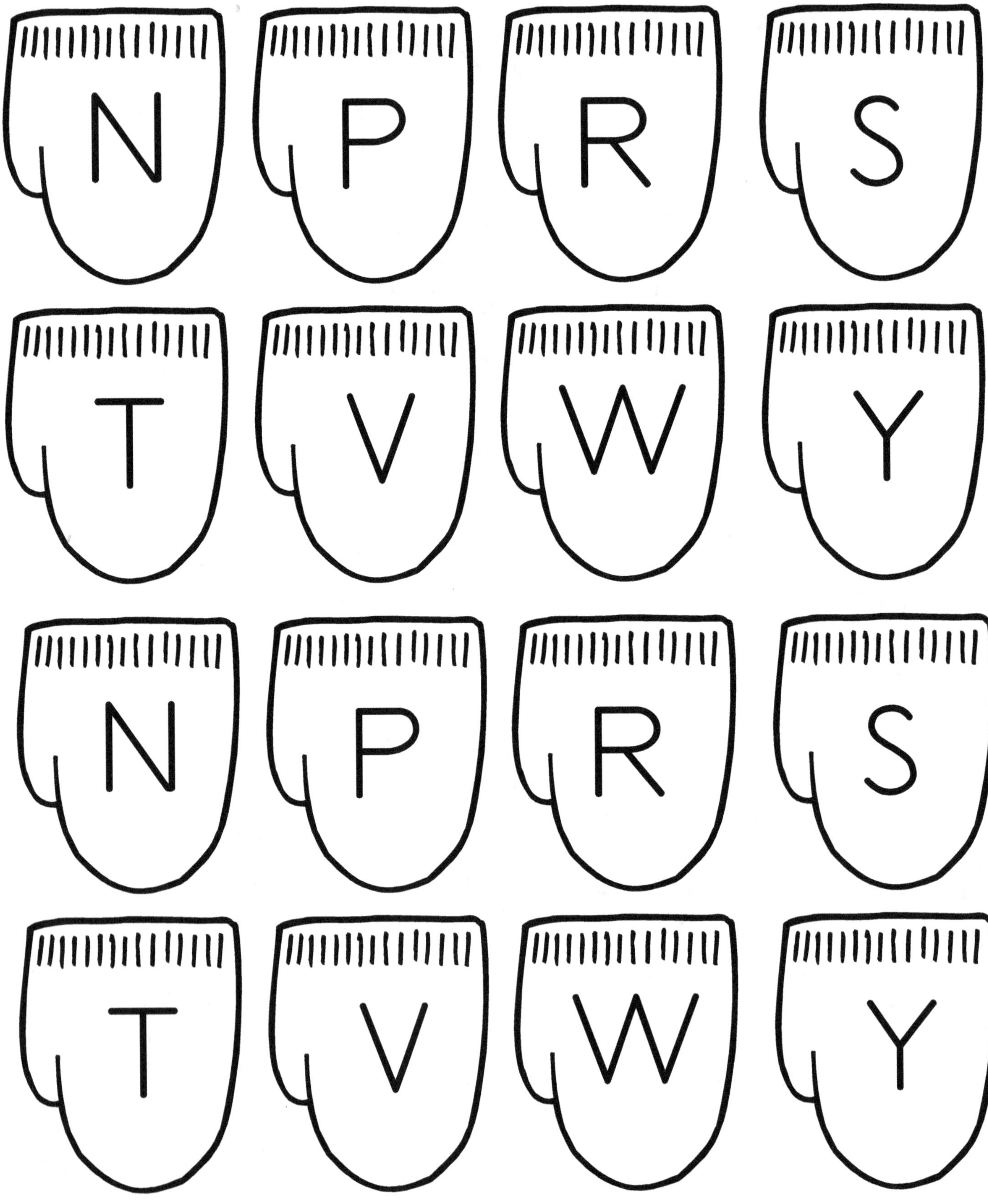

N P R S
T V W Y
N P R S
T V W Y

Reproduce, color, and cut out a set of game cards.

Mitten Game Cards

Beginning Sounds

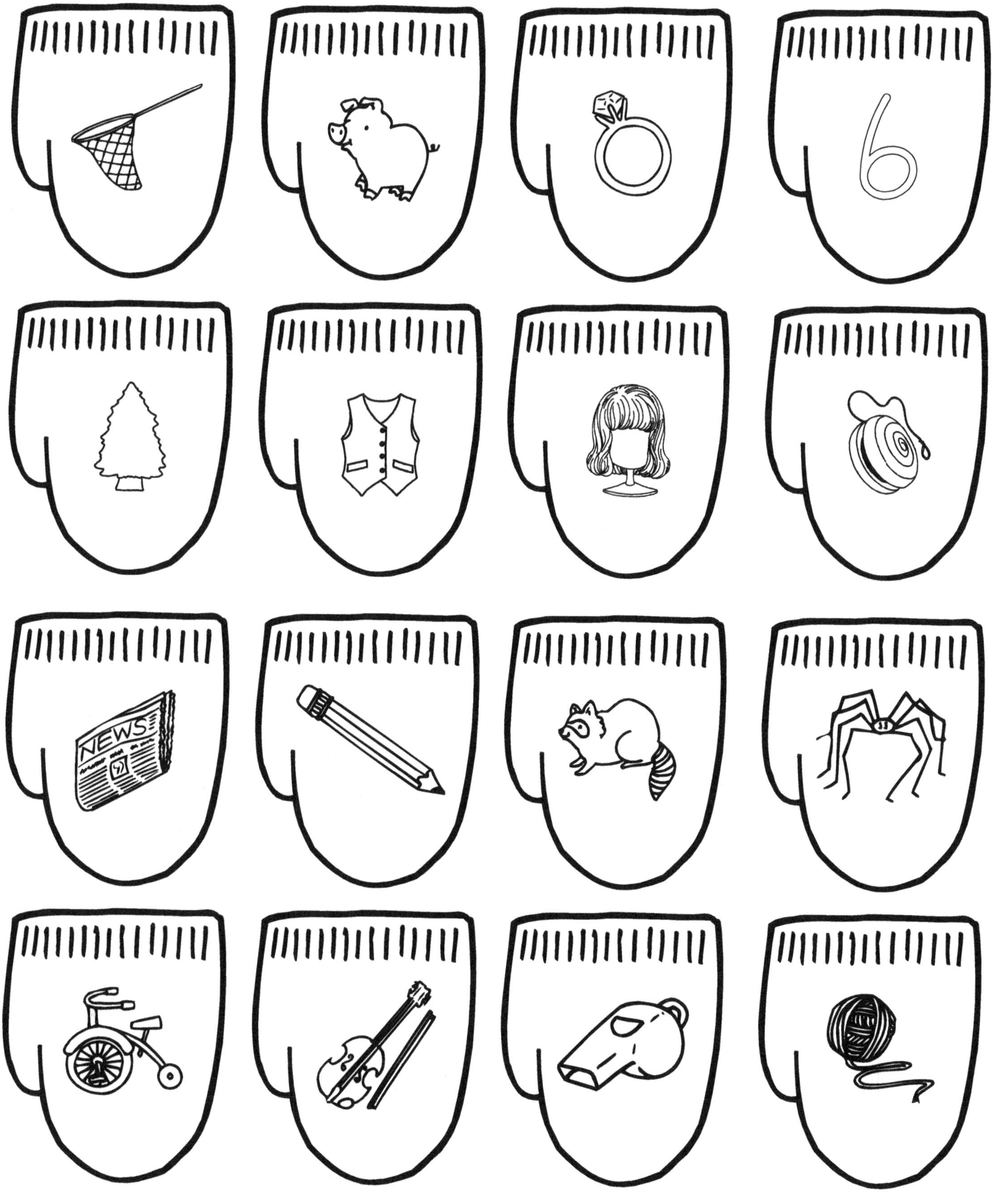

Reproduce, color, and cut out a set of game cards.

Mitten Game Cards
Ending Sounds

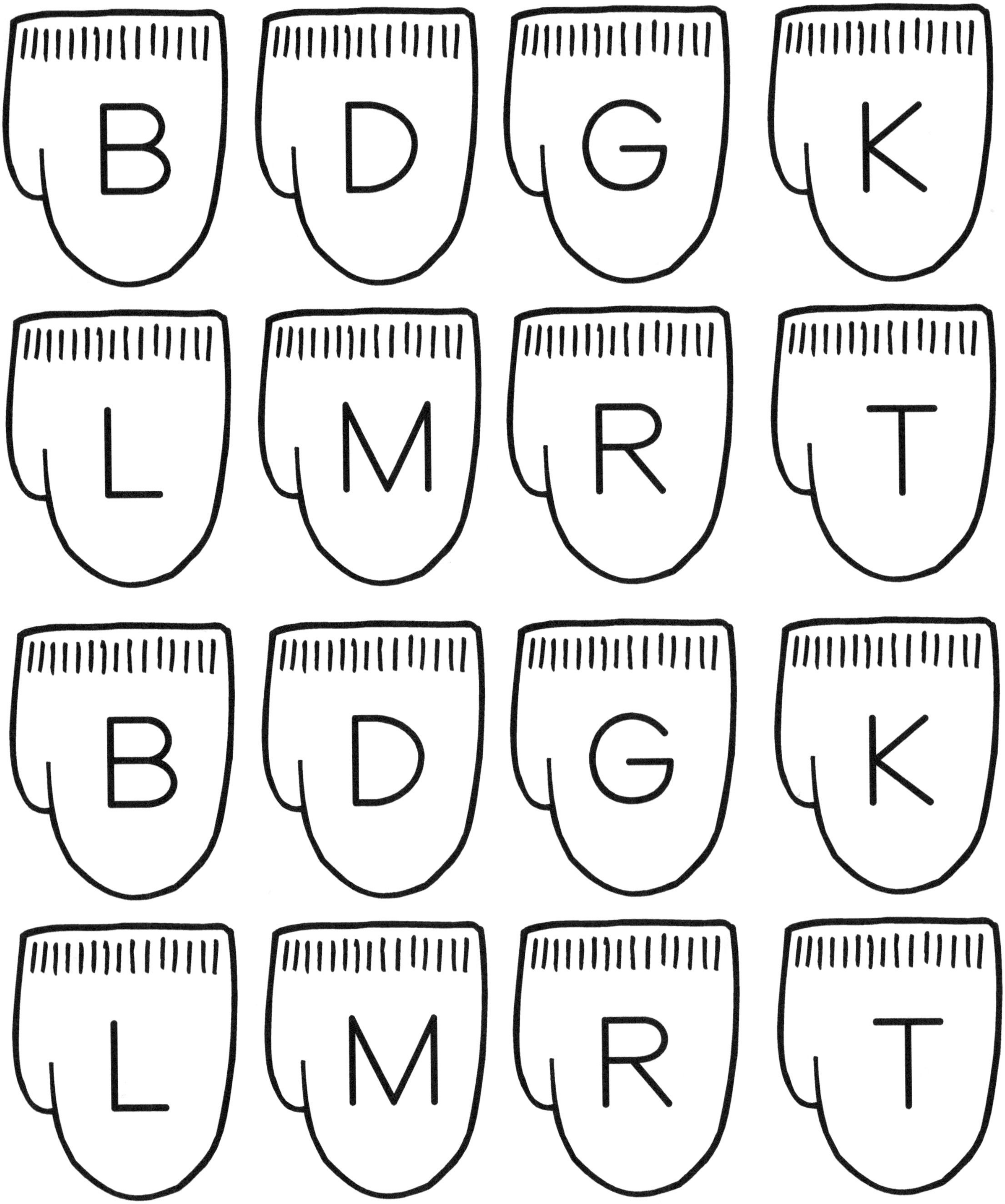

B D G K
L M R T
B D G K
L M R T

Reproduce, color, and cut out a set of game cards.

Mitten Game Cards

Ending Sounds

Reproduce, color, and cut out a set of game cards.

Pin A Tail On A Whale

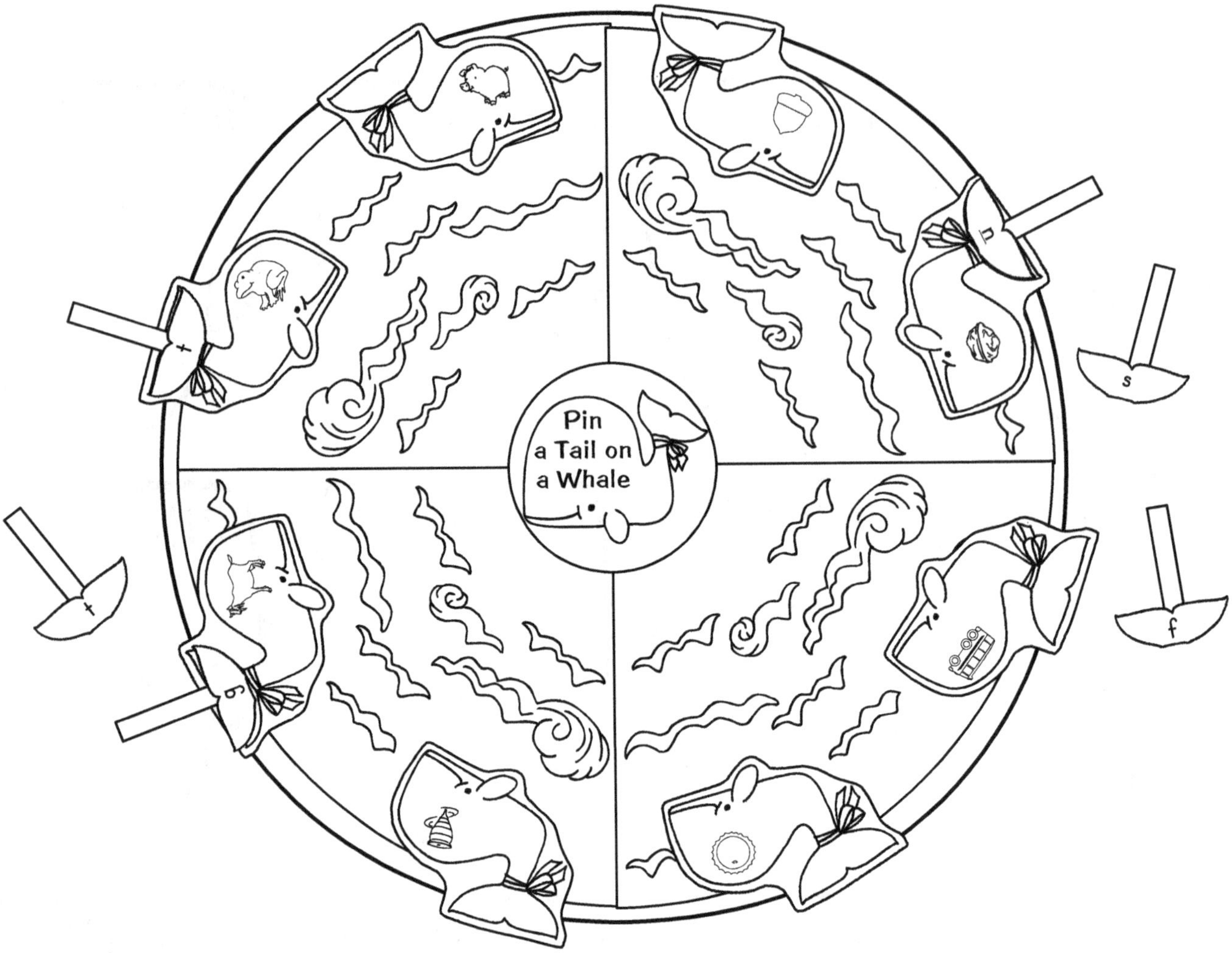

Materials
crayons, markers, scissors, glue, file folders, clothespins, large envelope

Assembly
Game Board: Reproduce, color, and cut out four game board patterns. Matching along the straight edges, glue the game board patterns on a poster board circle to form a round game board. Glue the title in the center of the game board. Then reproduce, color, cut out, and glue eight whale patterns on the assembled game board. Note: Make multiple game boards to focus on different beginning and ending sounds.

Clothespin Game Cards: Reproduce, color, and cut out a set of whale tail game cards. Glue a clothespin to the back of each game card. Decorate a large envelope with whale patterns. Store the clothespin game cards in the envelope.

How to Play
Set up the game board on a table. Players choose to practice beginning or ending sounds. Place the clothespin game cards, face down, on the table. Each player, in turn, draws a clothespin. If there is a match, the player identifies the match, and clips the clothespin to the correct whale. If there is no match, the player places the clothespin back on the table, face down. Play continues until a tail is attached to each matching whale on the game board.

Pin A Tail On A Whale Game Board and Title

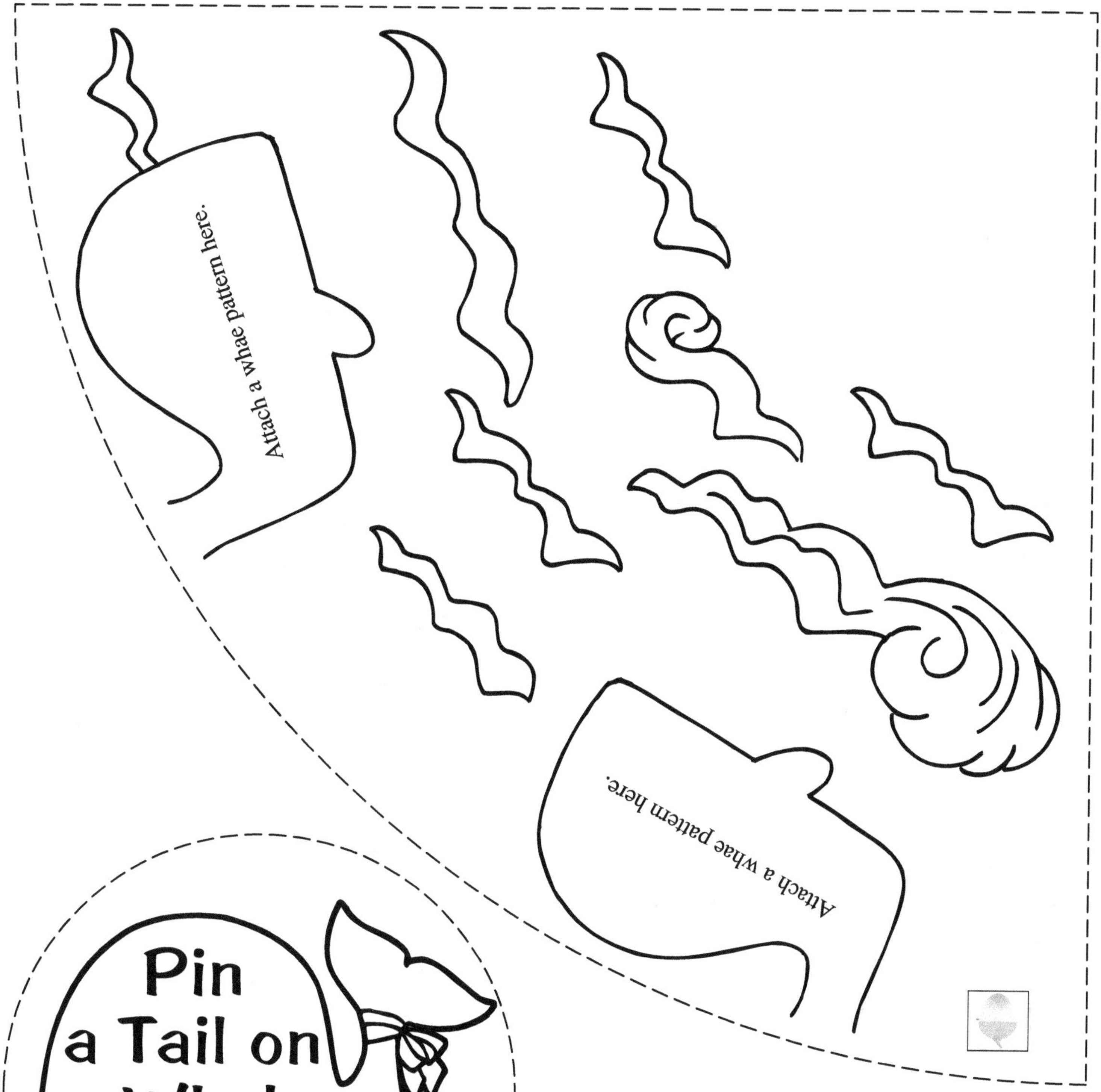

Attach a whale pattern here.

Attach a whale pattern here.

Pin a Tail on a Whale

Reproduce, color, cut out, and assemble four game board patterns on a poster board circle to form a round game board. Glue the title in the center of the game board.

Whale Patterns

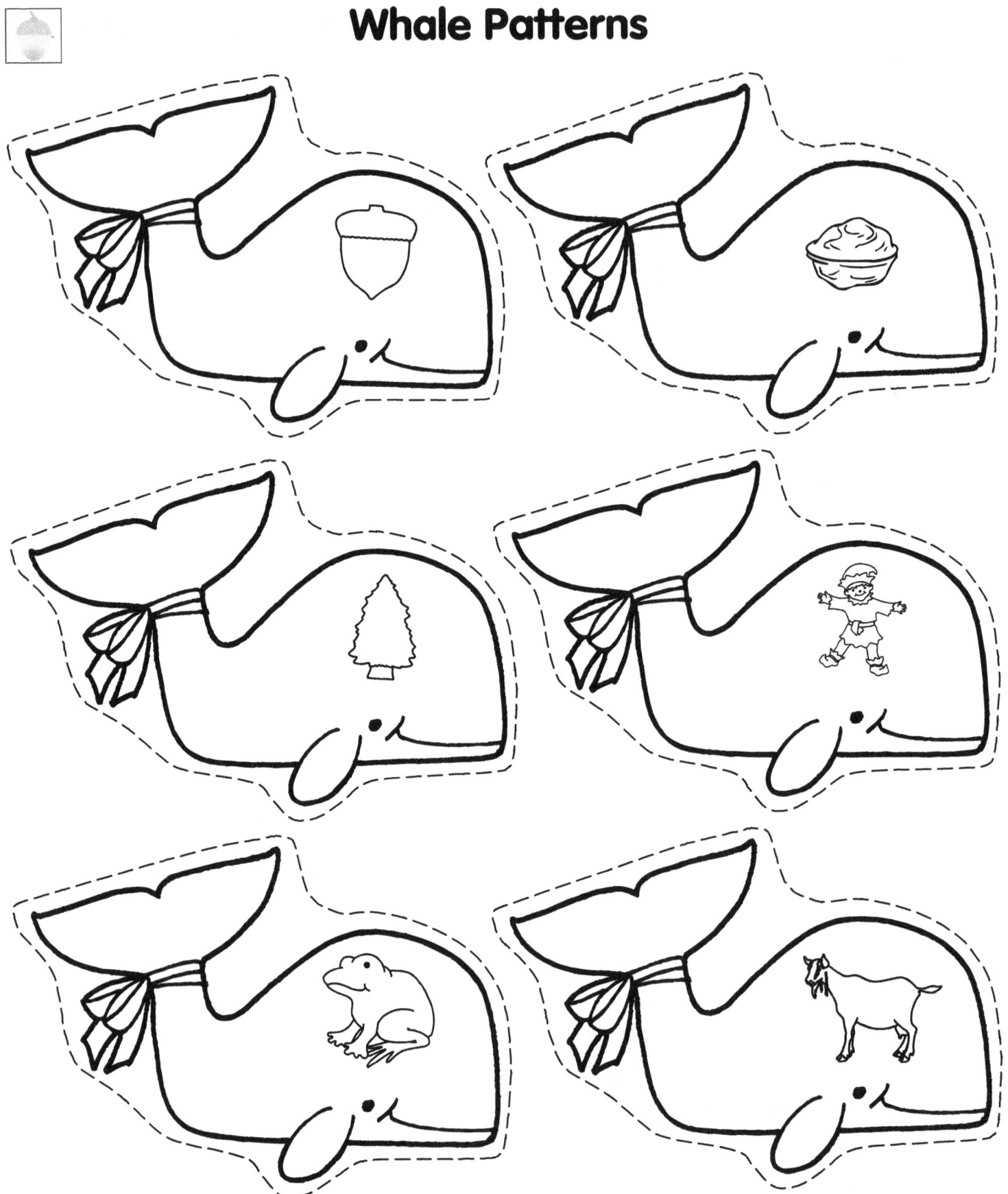

Reproduce, color, and cut out eight whale patterns. Glue the whale patterns around an assembled Pin A Tail On A Whale game board.

Whale Patterns

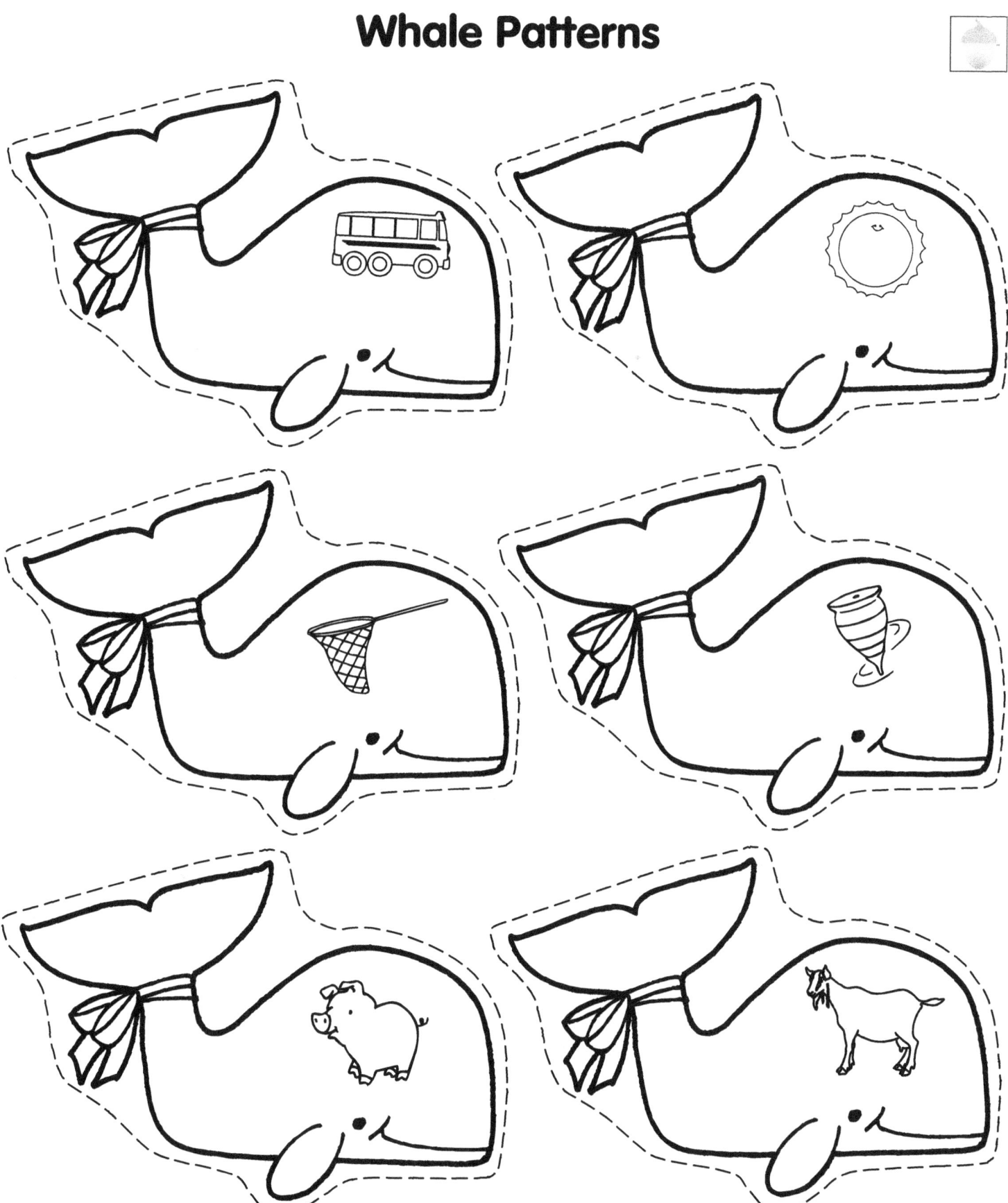

Creative Option: Make a Beginning Sounds Whale Pod chart. Draw waves on a sheet of poster board. Paint glue, then sprinkle glitter on the waves. White out, reproduce, and program a set of whale patterns with additional beginning sound pictures to accompany the whale patterns on pages 38 and 39. Reproduce, color, cut out, and glue the whale patterns on the poster board.

Whale Tail Game Cards

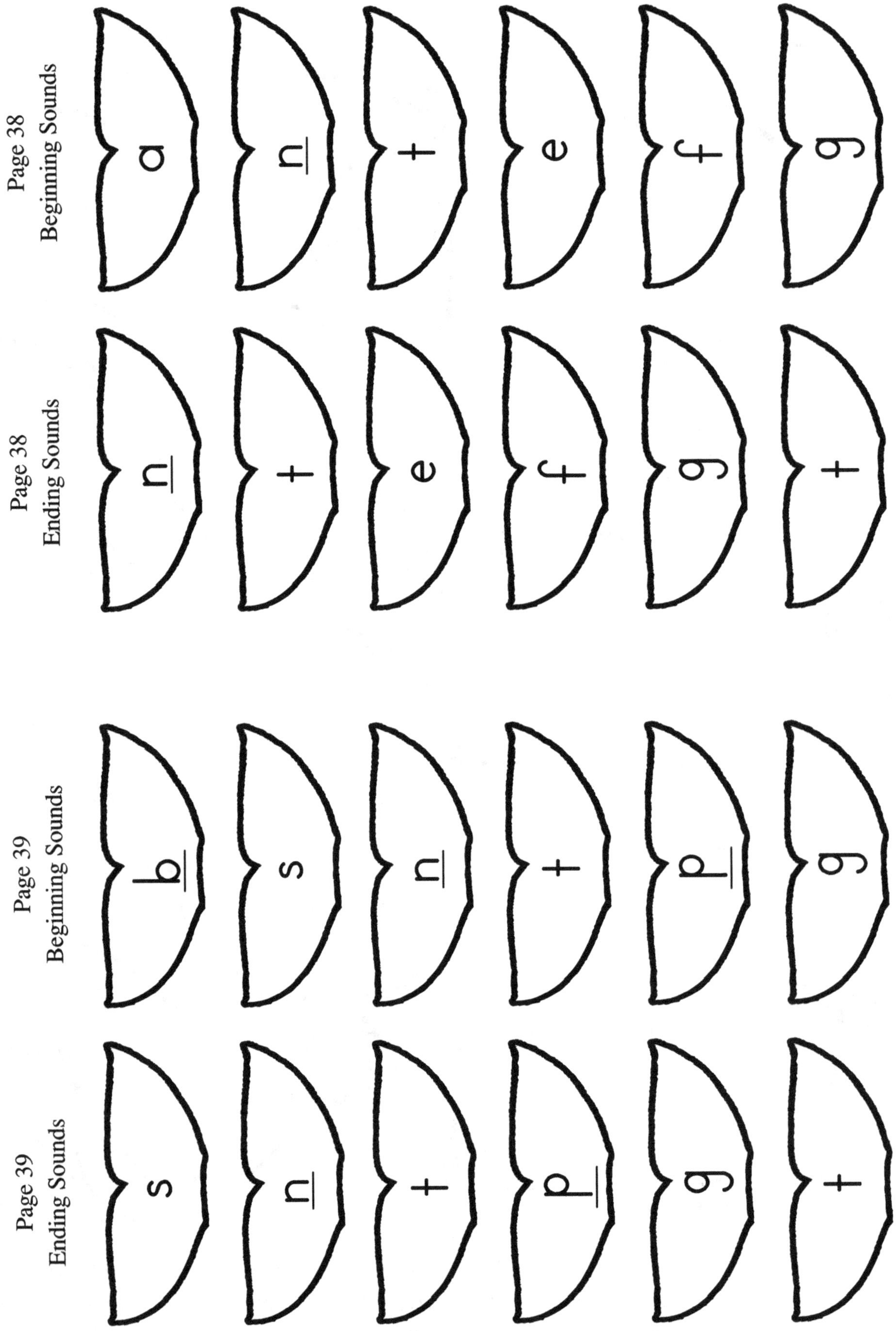

Page 38
Beginning Sounds: a, n, t, e, f, g

Page 38
Ending Sounds: n, t, e, f, g, t

Page 39
Beginning Sounds: b, s, n, t, p, g

Page 39
Ending Sounds: s, n, t, p, g, t

Reproduce, color, and cut out two sets of game cards.

There's a Mouse in the House
A Match Board Game
For Two Players

Materials
crayons, markers, scissors, glue, file folder, envelope

Assembly
Game Board: Reproduce, color, and cut out the cover and game board patterns. Glue each game board pattern to the inside of a folder. Glue the cover to the front of the folder, then laminate. Tape an envelope to the back of the game board folder to store game cards.

Game Cards: Reproduce, color, laminate, then cut out three sets of game cards. Option: Reproduce, color, and glue each page of game cards to the back of a sheet of gift wrap, then laminate and cut out the cards. Store the game cards in the envelope on the back of the game board folder.

How to Play
Set up the game board on a table. One player shuffles and places the mouse game cards, face down, on the table. Each player, in turn, draws a card. If there is a match, the player identifies the match, and places the card on the correct picture mouse. If there is no match, the player places the card, face down, in a discard pile. Play continues until a letter mouse has been placed on each picture mouse on the game board. Reshuffle cards if needed.

There's a Mouse in the House Game Board

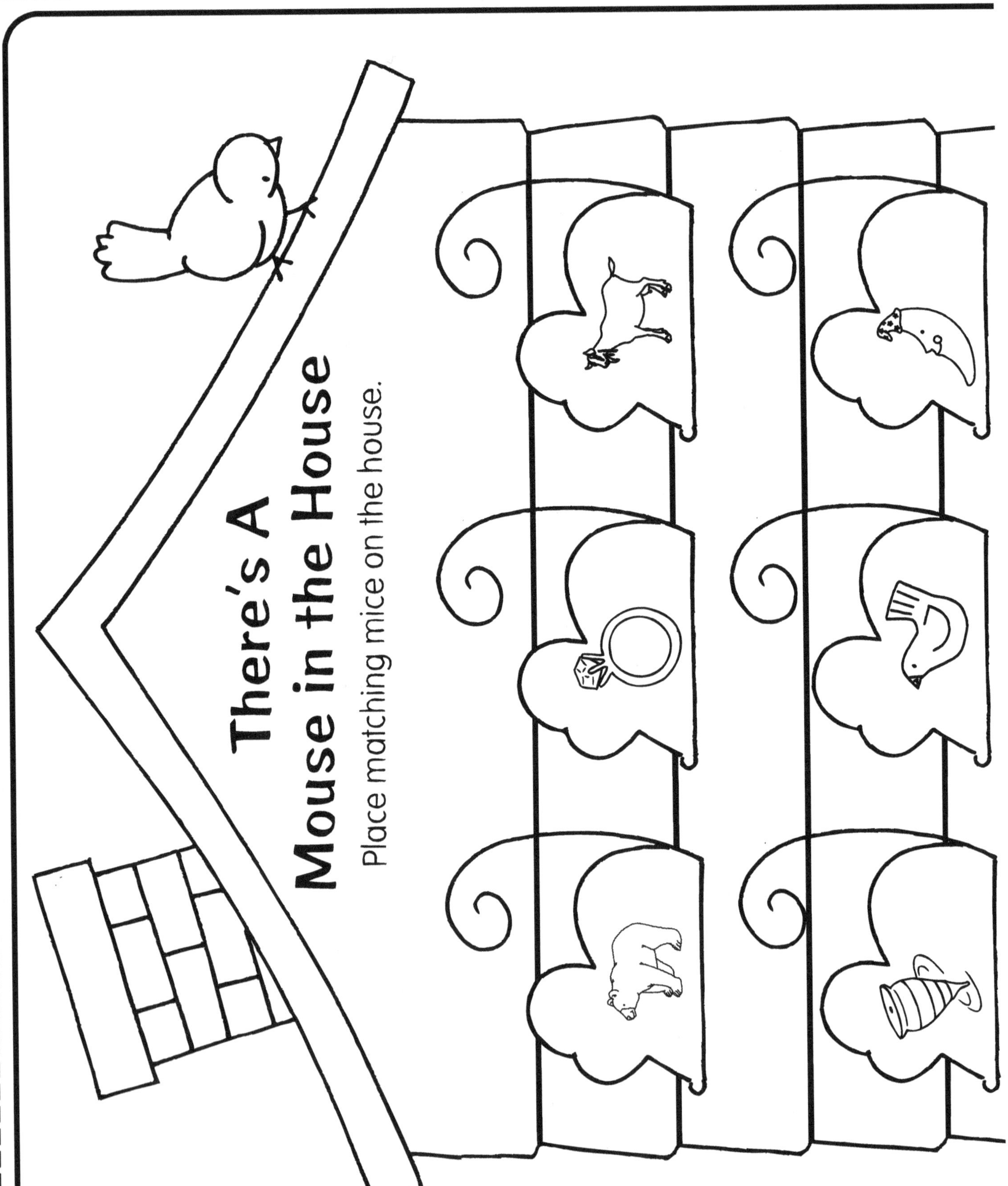

There's A Mouse in the House

Place matching mice on the house.

There's a Mouse in the House Game Board

Mouse Game Cards

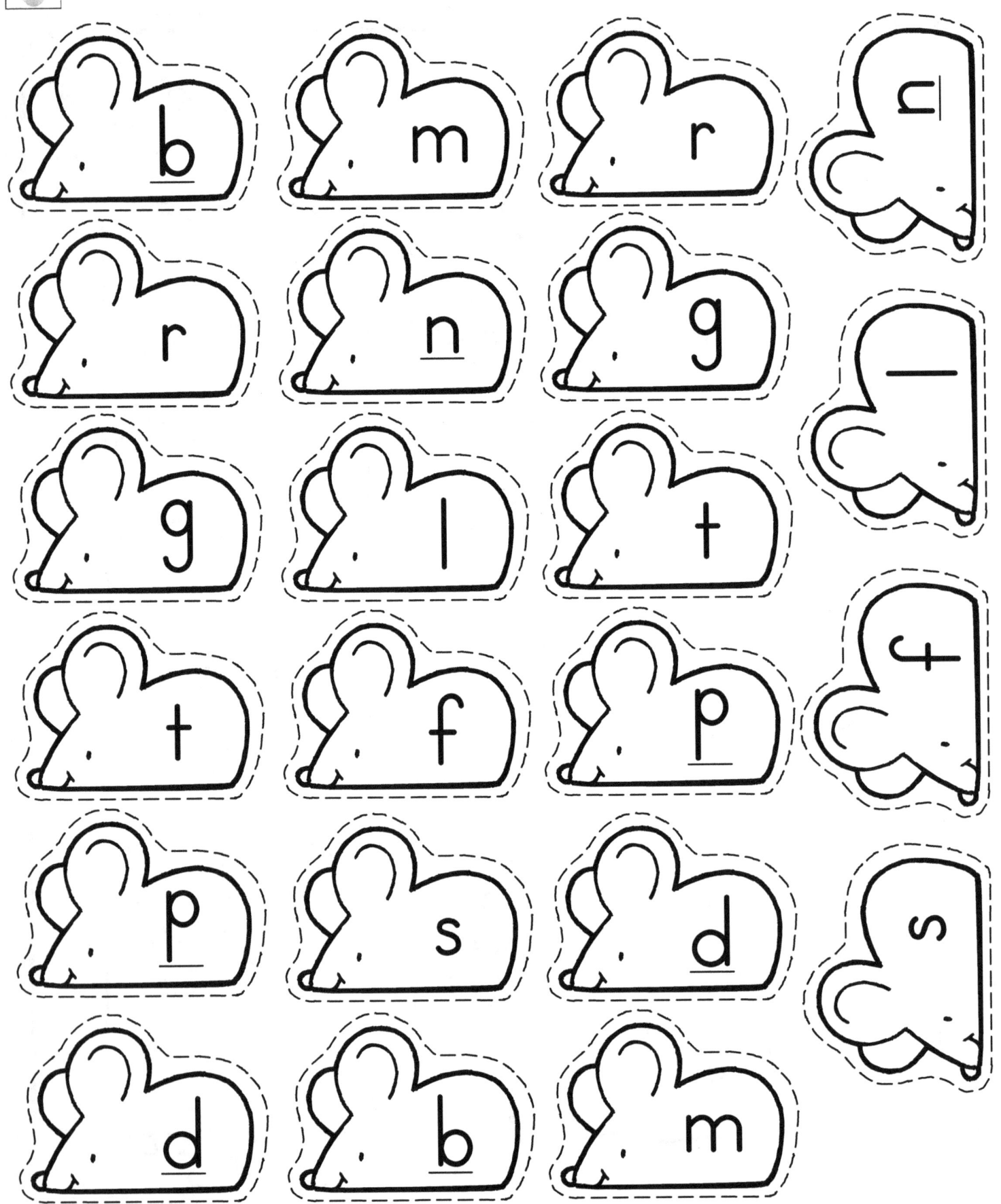

Reproduce, color, and cut out three sets of game cards.

There's a Mouse in the House Cover

There's A Mouse in the House

Mud Puddle Piglets
A Match Board Game
For Two Players

Materials

crayons, markers, scissors, glue, file folder, envelope

Assembly

Game Board: Reproduce, color, and cut out the cover and game board patterns. Matching in the center, glue the game board patterns to the inside of a folder. Glue the cover to the front of the folder, then laminate. Tape an envelope to the back of the game board folder to store game cards. Write "Beginning Sound Practice" or "Ending Sound Practice" on each folder. Note: Make several game boards to utilize all of the mud puddle game cards. Reproduce, color, cut out, and glue a different set of mud puddle pictures on the piglets on each game board. For "Ending Sound Practice," glue a "t" over the "c" on the cover.

Game Cards: Reproduce, color, laminate, then cut out the mud puddle letter and word game cards. Option: Reproduce, color, and glue a page of game cards to the back of a sheet of gift wrap, then laminate and cut apart the cards. Store the game cards in the envelope on the back of the game board folder.

How to Play

Set up a beginning or ending sound game board and matching mud puddle cards on a table. Tell children if the game is a beginning or ending sound activity. One player shuffles and places the cards, face down, on the table. Each player, in turn, draws, and identifies the individual letter or sounds out the first or last letter of the word on the card. If there is a match, he or she places the letter or word card next to the matching picture on the game board. If there is no match, the player places the card, face down, in a discard pile. Play continues until there is a matching mud puddle letter and word on each piglet pattern.

Mud Puddle Piglets Cover

Mud Puddle Piglets

c   cat

Mud Puddle Piglets Game Board

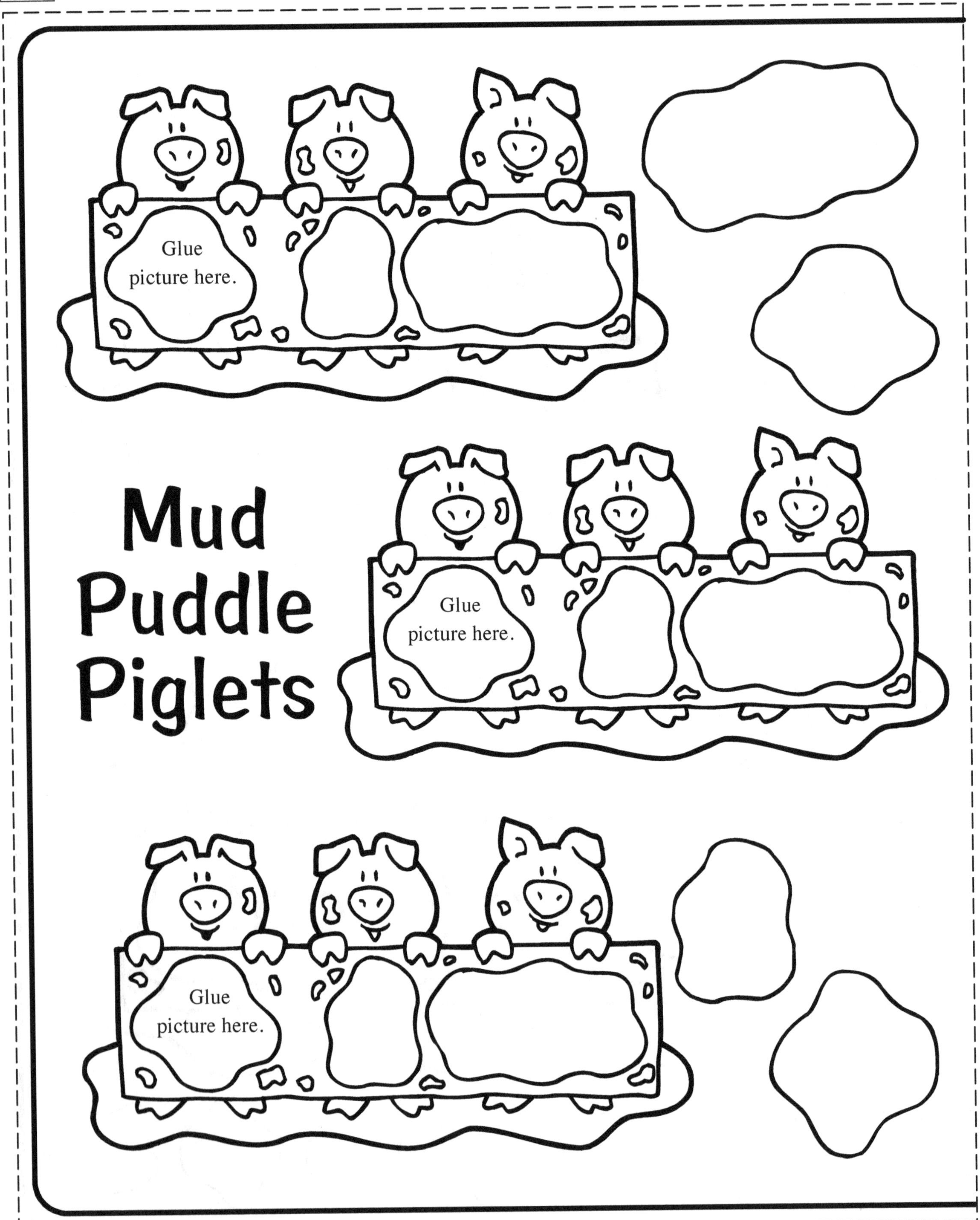

Glue picture here.

Mud Puddle Piglets

Glue picture here.

Glue picture here.

Mud Puddle Piglets Game Board

Place a matching mud puddle letter and word next to each picture.

Mud Puddle Game Cards

	b	l	ball	pen	mop
	b	d	bed	n	p
	c	r	car	p	m
	d	g	dog		
	s	x	six	drum	net
	d	k	duck	m	t
	r	g	ring	d	n
	w	g	wig		

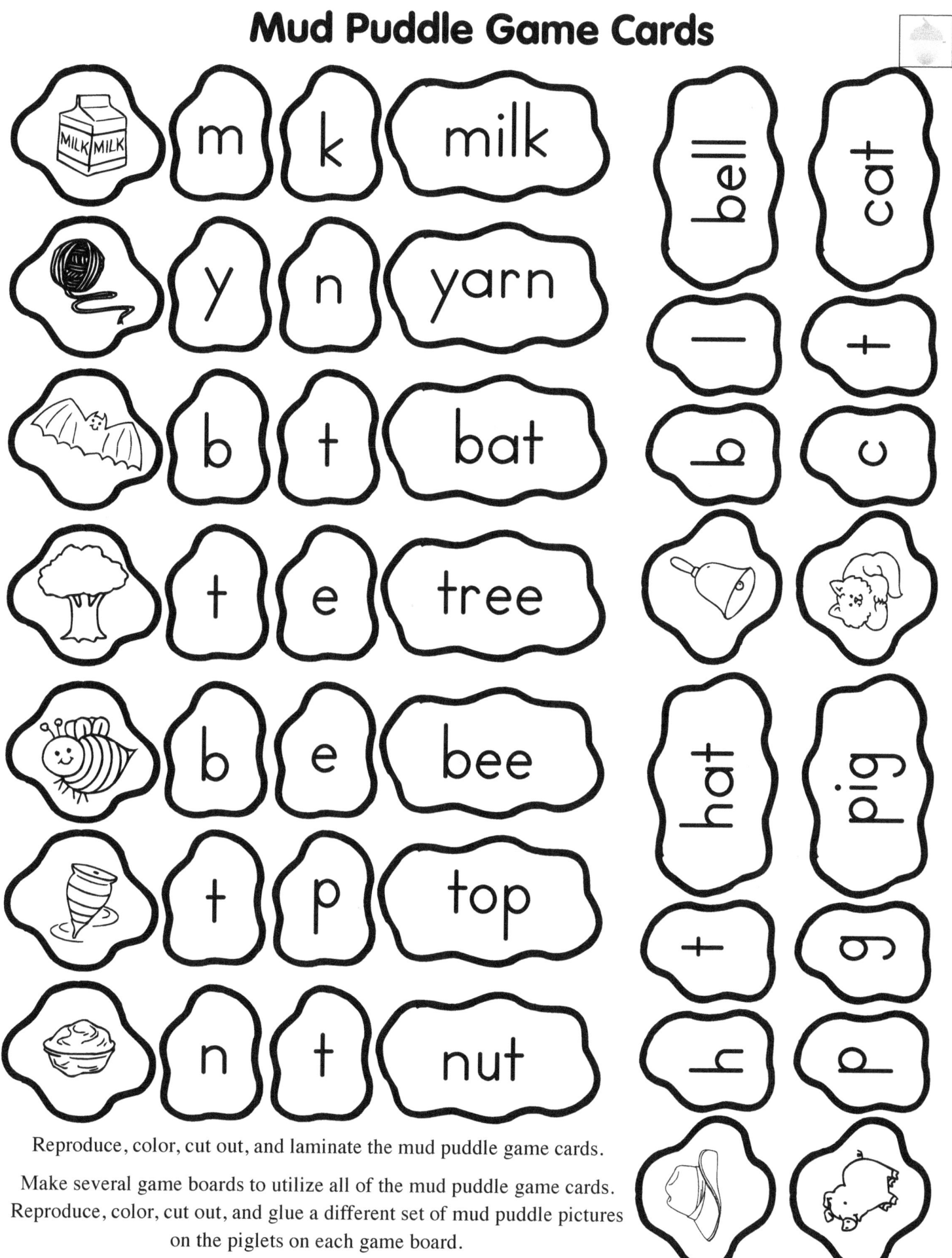

The King's Crowns
A Match Board Game
For Two Players

Materials
crayons, markers, scissors, glue, file folder, envelope

Assembly
Game Board: Reproduce, color, and cut out the cover and game board patterns. Glue each game board pattern to the inside of a folder. Reproduce, color, cut out, and glue six jewel bands on each game board. Glue the cover to the front of the folder, then laminate. Tape an envelope to the back of the game board folder to store game cards. Note: Make multiple game boards to focus on different words. Option: Provide wipe-off crayons for children to write in the letters.

Game Cards: Reproduce, color, laminate, then cut apart one set of jewel game cards. Option: Reproduce, color, and glue each page of game cards to the back of a sheet of gift wrap, then laminate and cut apart the cards. Store the game cards in the envelope on the back of the game board folder.

How to Play
Set up the game board on a table. Each player chooses to play one side of the game board. One player shuffles and places the jewel cards, face down, on the table. Each player, in turn, draws a card. If there is a match, the player identifies the match and places the beginning or ending sound jewel on the correct crown. If there is no match, the player places the card, face down, in a discard pile. Play continues until each player has placed a beginning and ending sound jewel on each crown on his or her game board. Reshuffle cards if needed.

The King's Crowns Cover

The King's Crowns

The King's Crowns Game Board

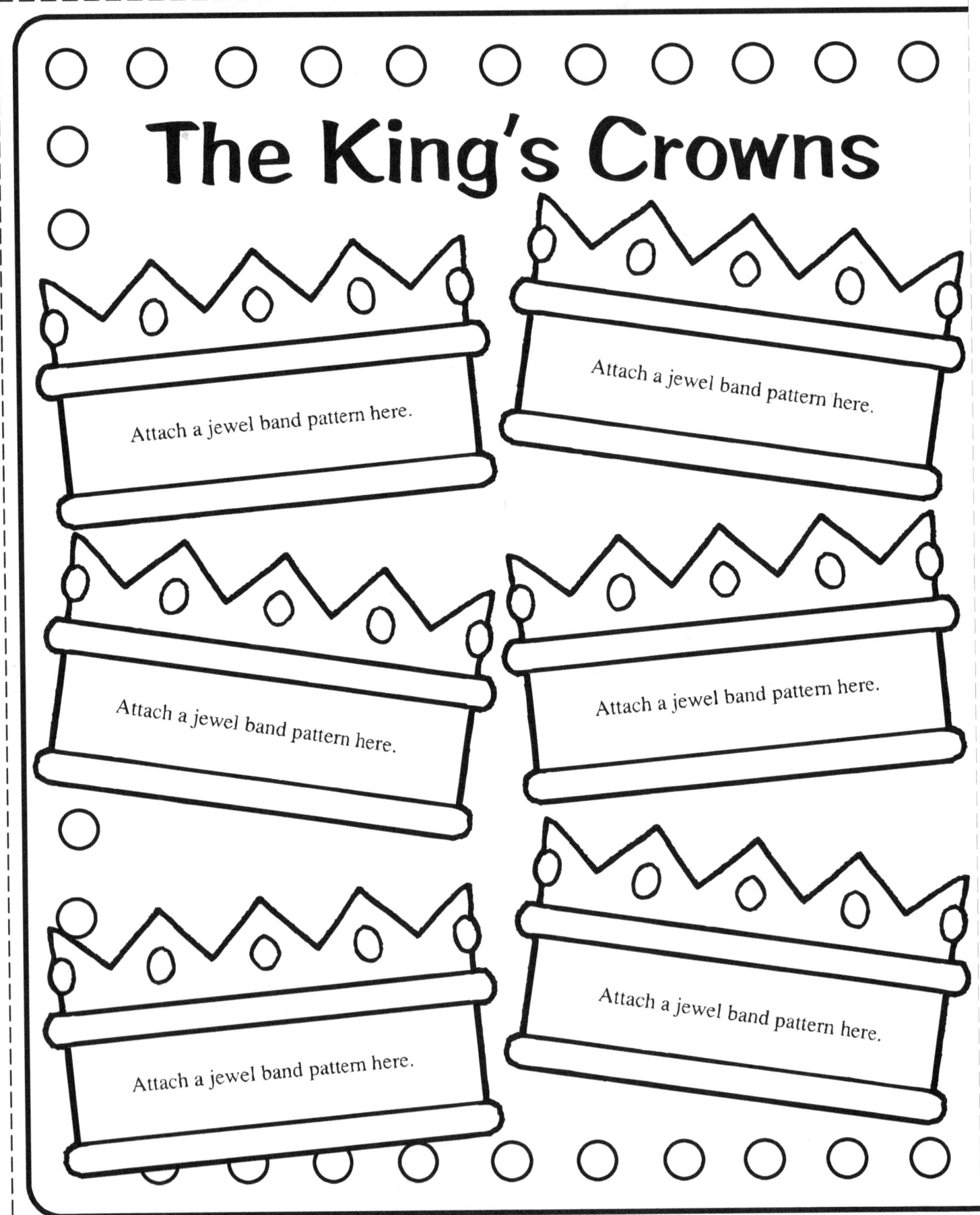

The King's Crowns Game Board

Place the matching jewels on each crown.

Attach a jewel band pattern here.

Attach a jewel band pattern here.

Attach a jewel band pattern here.

Attach a jewel band pattern here.

Attach a jewel band pattern here.

Attach a jewel band pattern here.

Jewel Bands and Game Cards

Jewel Bands · Beginning Sounds · Ending Sounds

				Beginning Sounds	Ending Sounds
🚌		u		b	s
🏏		a		b	t
🐝		e		b	e
👶		i		b	b

Ending Sounds: | x | d | t | p | r | g | f | g |

Beginning Sounds: | b | b | c | c | c | d | e | e |

Jewel Bands: | o | e | a | u | a | o | l | g |

Reproduce, color, and cut apart one set of jewel bands. Glue a jewel band on each crown inside the game board.

Jewel Bands and Game Cards

Jewel Bands				Beginning Sounds	Ending Sounds
🦊		o		f	x
👒		a		h	t
🧴		n		i	k
🍨		u		n	t

Ending Sounds	t	g	x	n	n	p	b	g
Beginning Sounds	n	p	s	s	t	t	w	w
Jewel Bands	e	i	i	u	e	o	e	i
	🥅	🐷	🪱	⭕	10	 🔔	 🕸️	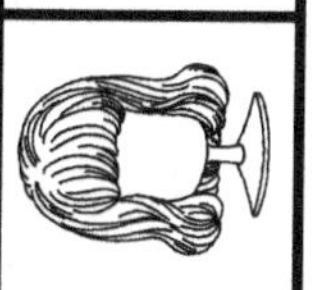 💇

Creative Option: Enlarge, reproduce, color, cut apart, and glue each jewel band on an oak tag sentence strip. Laminate each oak tag strip. Provide wipe-off crayons for a writing practice activity.

Can Stackers
A Stacker Game
For One to Two Players

Materials
crayons, markers, scissors, glue, file folder, envelope

Assembly
Game Board: Reproduce, color, and cut out the cover and the can stackers game board patterns. Glue each game board pattern to the inside of a folder. Decorate the front of the folder with game card cutouts, then laminate. Tape an envelope to the back of the game board folder to store game cards.

Game Cards: Reproduce, color, laminate, then cut apart two sets of game cards. Option: Reproduce, color, and glue each page of game cards to the back of a sheet of gift wrap, then laminate and cut apart the cards. Store the game cards in the envelope on the back of the game board folder.

How to Play
Set up the stacker game and cards on a table. Each player chooses a game board to play. Then one player shuffles and places the card deck, face down, on the table. Each player, in turn, draws, and stacks a game card on the matching space on the game board. Play continues until all the cards have been played. Matches include beginning or ending sounds, words, or pictures. Each space has four correct matches.

Option: Use the game cards to play a game of Concentration. Shuffle and place all the cards, face down, on a table. Each player, in turn, turns over any two cards to find a match. If the player finds a match, he or she takes the cards and the next player takes a turn. If there is no match, each card is turned back over in the same position. Play continues until all the cards are taken.

Can Stackers Game Board

Can Stackers

Stack the matching cans.

Can Stackers Game Board

Can Stackers

Stack the matching cans.

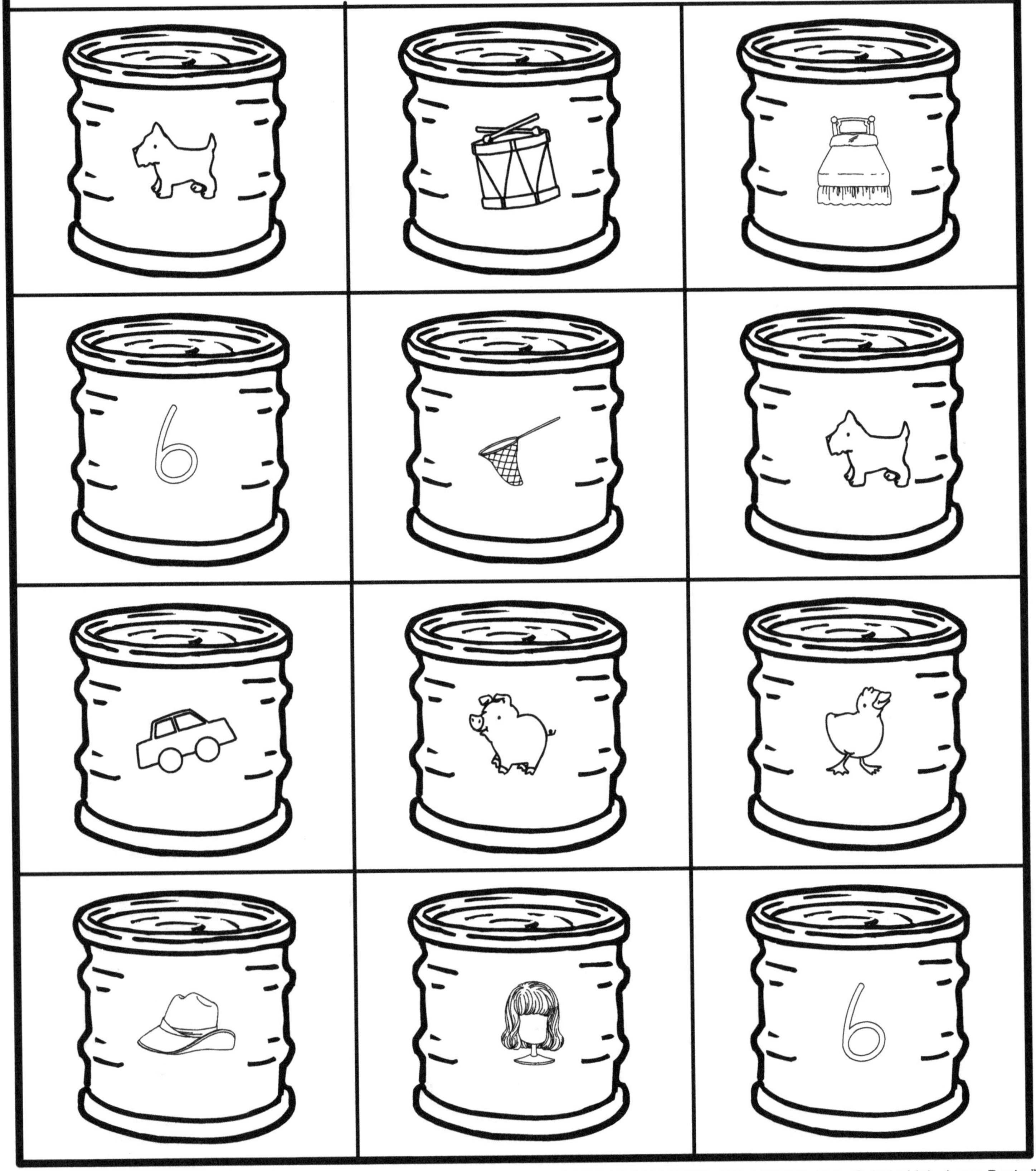

Can Game Cards

Creative Option: Reproduce, color, and cut out a set of cans.
Cut out and glue pictures of different food items from magazine or grocery flyers on the cans.
Children can practice sorting the cans by beginning sounds, ending sounds, or food groups.

Can Game Cards

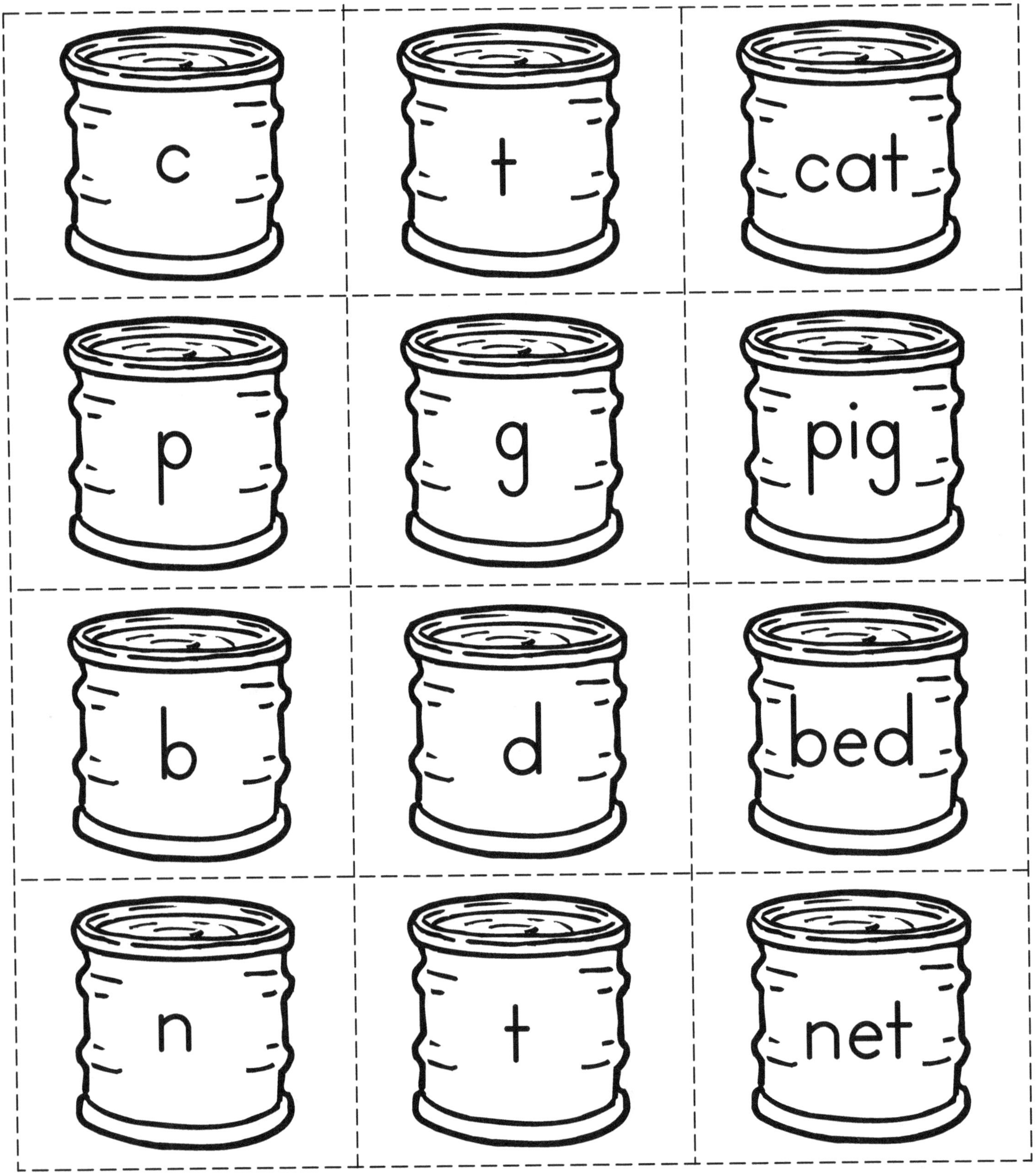

c	t	cat
p	g	pig
b	d	bed
n	t	net

Can Game Cards

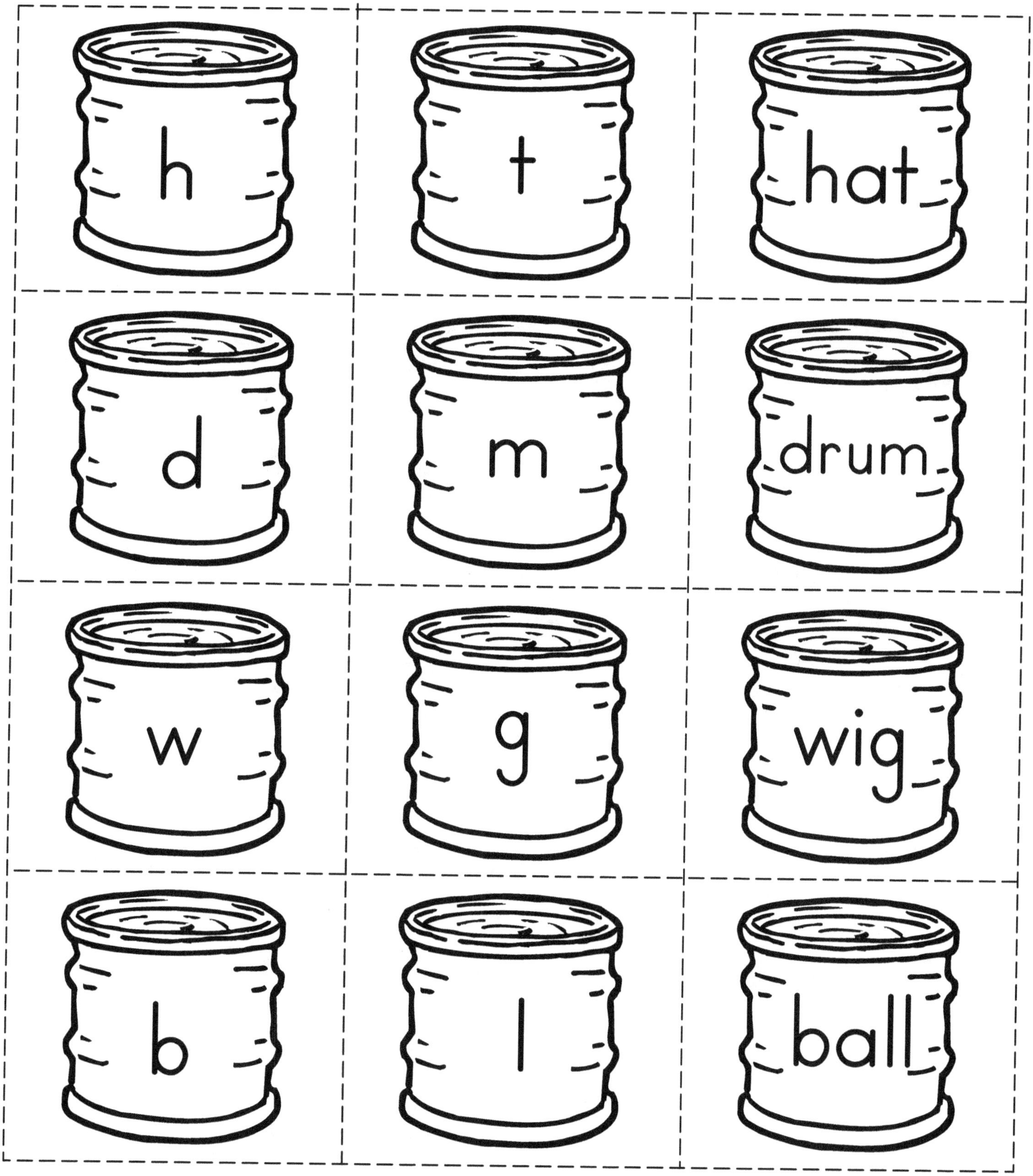

h	t	hat
d	m	drum
w	g	wig
b	l	ball

Can Game Cards

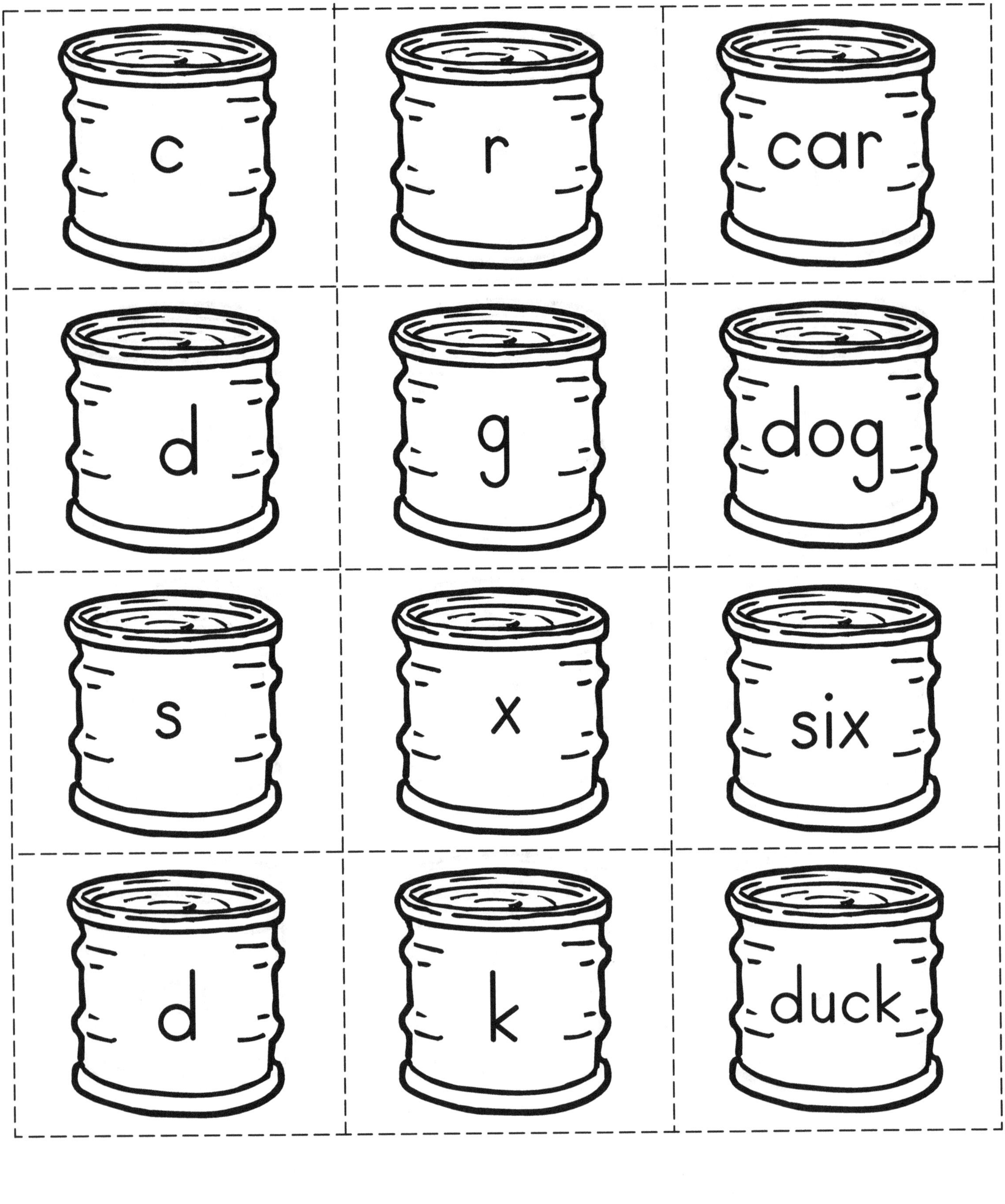

c	r	car
d	g	dog
s	x	six
d	k	duck

Little Acorn Books™

Promoting Early Skills for a Lifetime™

A Hands-on Picture Book Series • Infancy–Age 4

Miss Pitty Pat & Friends
Preschool–Grade 1

Using Crayons, Scissors, & Glue for Crafts
Preschool–Grade 1

Mookie's Christmas Tree
For All Ages and Not Just for Christmas

Little Acorn Books™
Visit our web site:
www.littleacornbooks.com

LAB201312 • ONCE UPON A TIME • 978-1-937257-47-7 • © 2014 Little Acorn Books™

www.ingramcontent.com/pod-product-compliance
Lightning Source LLC
Chambersburg PA
CBHW081021040426
42444CB00014B/3298